Praise for *The Politics of Promotion*

"More than a 'rah rah' motivational treatise, *The Politics of Promotion* sends a strong message that we must work hard AND be smart as women in today's organizations. I found women's leadership guru Bonnie Marcus's blend of personal experience, relevant examples, and applicable tools to be a goldmine. Her strategic networking templates alone are worth the price of the book. A meaty great read for all women and those who support them."

—Jennifer B. Kahnweiler,
PhD, CSP, author of *Quiet Influence*
and *The Introverted Leader*

"*The Politics of Promotion* is packed with practical knowledge every woman needs in clear, engaging, and actionable language. Marcus outlines a proven method for women to navigate the complexities of the workplace and get the promotions they deserve."

—Gloria Feldt,
cofounder and President,
Take the Lead; and author of *No Excuses*

"Women tend to perceive office politics as something distasteful. *The Politics of Promotion* is a very helpful book for individuals needing to better understand and embrace the importance of company politics, not only as a critical part of career advancement, but also as a more effective way to successfully carry out your daily job responsibilities. Bonnie Marcus's research demonstrates how being political savvy allows you to build important relationships with critical stakeholders who may be able to support, mentor, and promote you. Reading this book will help you to learn how to navigate across an organization to achieve your career and business goals by working with and through others."

—Alexandra Glucksmann,
COO, Editas Medicine

"Women are graduating from college and entering the workforce ill prepared to navigate their new environment. Putting your head down and achieving great results works in school, but being successful in your career requires more. Bonnie Marcus has nailed the missing piece: political savvy. *The Politics of Promotion* should be required reading for all college graduates."

—Tiffany Dufu,
Chief Leadership Officer,
The Levo League

"Women regularly think that doing a great job ensures promotion—I used to think so, too. Instead, we know from data and personal experience that performance excellence means, at most, that you might be considered; actually securing the promotion requires a great deal more. Bonnie Marcus has seen how this plays across multiple disciplines and industries, and is full of insight and advice that will put women in a far stronger position to understand how to create the opportunities their talent demands. Her tough love acknowledges injustice, but her tough thinking is what promises success."

—Margaret Heffernan,
author of *Willful Blindness* and *A Bigger Prize*

"Until genuine meritocracy becomes the norm, women will continue to face subtle bias and double standards. They will be greatly helped in navigating the traps and blind alleys of organizational life by the career advice that Bonnie Marcus offers in this readable book. Bonnie reframes the 'dirty' words of politics, networking, and self-promotion as necessary leadership skills that can achieve all-round benefits when exercised thoughtfully. Ambitious readers will feel better equipped to go for the leadership prize."

—Alison Maitland,
coauthor of *Future Work* and
Why Women Mean Business

"Bonnie Marcus shares from her experience on how to get the recognition and rewards you deserve for your work by managing the interpersonal dynamics of the workplace. Politics is inherent in all human relationships. *The Politics of Promotion* will teach you how to interact professionally and get promoted while staying true to yourself."

—Marilyn Tam,
author of *The Happiness Choice*

THE POLITICS OF PROMOTION

THE POLITICS OF PROMOTION

HOW HIGH-ACHIEVING WOMEN GET AHEAD AND STAY AHEAD

BONNIE MARCUS

Bonnie Marcus

WILEY

With love to my children,
Abby and Tim

Contents

Contents

Introduction

You work really hard. You have what it takes to do a good job. All your skills and education have prepared you to have a successful career. You are passionate about what you do. You enjoy your colleagues, and you invest a great deal of time and energy into every project to make sure it's perfect.

Perhaps you have been recognized for your top performance. You think you are well on your way to getting a promotion. There is a new opportunity to move up. It would mean more compensation and more responsibility, and you are ready to take it on. You apply for the position. You know you are qualified, maybe even overqualified, and you are confident that the job will be yours. And then the bottom falls out. Someone else is chosen over you, and that person isn't nearly as qualified as you are! You are frustrated and angry. You feel betrayed. Wow! You didn't see it coming.

What happened? Politics!

Workplaces are highly political environments where decisions about who gets ahead, who gets more compensation, and who gets access to scarce resources are not based on performance alone. Our naïve assumption that our performance will guarantee a successful career is a dangerous one. This assumption results in thousands of women being blindsided. And it happens every day.

Where does this assumption come from? As young girls, we are taught academic success is a must. Don't you remember what a great feeling it was to come home with a good report card and have your mom and dad tell you how proud they were? I recall it well. Receiving good grades was important, and I worked hard to excel in school. I wasn't even sure what I wanted to be when I grew up, but I got the message that doing well in school was necessary for me to be successful in whatever I chose to do in life.

Success in school is based on industriousness. You work diligently, study, and prepare, and you are rewarded with good grades. This belief and behavior, however, does not translate to the workplace.

Early in my career, I worked for a national health care organization. I joined this company as a regional manager and after eight years worked my way up to area vice president. I was a rock star! I won every top-performance award for my region and loved the work and the people I worked with. So I wasn't terribly concerned when we started to hear rumors about reorganization. I had survived a couple of mergers and acquisitions and had always landed on top.

The reorganization became a reality, and one day we had a conference call with the CEO to announce the changes. There were two ways this would impact me. First, there were some changes in the structure of my region, and a new vice president role was created. Second, I had a new boss, a buddy of the CEO from outside the company and another industry.

I was excited about the possibility of a promotion to vice president. I asked for the promotion. I lobbied for the job. All of my 18 direct reports called the new SVP and recommended he choose me. I was confident the job was mine.

And then I was blindsided. The vice president position went to someone else from outside my region. I was devastated, angry, and frustrated. After investing eight years of my time, energy, and talent, I had been overlooked. I felt betrayed.

What else did I need to do to move up? I had a history of great performance, and I had worked the politics to some degree. After all, I had asked my new boss for the promotion. I had talked to my direct reports to let them know I was interested in the new position. Many of them recommended me for the job. I thought I had done everything right. But did I?

No!

I learned many lessons as a result of this experience. I learned that I was very naïve. I learned that focusing on my work alone was a mistake. I learned that understanding the way decisions are made in your organization is critical. It is essential to know who has the power and influence over the decisions that impact your career. And it is paramount to build allies and champions across the organization.

I failed to build a relationship with my new boss because I didn't like him. I didn't understand how the decision about the vice president position would be made. I didn't understand the politics.

In the workplace, the rules of the game are not as simple as you'd think. Although hard work and performance are important, they are not the sole basis for advancement. Yes, your track record is critical, but unlike school, the workplace has different criteria for success. Often promotions are based on personality, on the ability to engage in the organization's politics and promote oneself with intention, and to network and build relationships.

Can you see what happens when we ignore these things? We are still working on an assumption that helped us reach academic success. We behave as if this assumption is valid. But it doesn't help us in the workplace. In fact, it works against us and sets us up to be blindsided.

Potential land mines for women are everywhere. We would like to believe that gender bias has dissipated, but many organizations now have a subtle form of bias that is much more challenging to anticipate and navigate. This unconscious bias adds to the complexity women face when navigating the political landscape. This is why this book is so important. While it's true that both genders need to embrace the culture and politics of their organization, women face different challenges. Due to their exclusion from the inner networks of power and influence, unconscious bias can ambush them at any time.

I have written this book because I believe wholeheartedly that women must get savvy about workplace politics if they are serious about their careers. We need to get serious, not only because we deserve it, but also because companies need the expertise and perspective of both genders. Sure, there has been a lot of research and discussion about the challenges we face as women in attaining leadership positions. But I know, and I'm certain you do as well, that we have the talent to lead and that our leadership helps organizations prosper.

We need to be at the table! We need to be there because we bring value and a unique viewpoint, but getting a seat is still complicated for women. There are people in your organization with different agendas and allegiances that you need to understand in order to be successful. Political savvy is about relationships and a focus on what others think and feel. It's about aligning yourself with key stakeholders and building relationships of trust and influence. You need these relationships in order to thrive. You need information about the politics of your workplace in order to survive! It's important to understand that attaining a leadership position not only helps your career but also helps your company.

For those of you who have missed out on a promotion, this book is for you. For those of you who still believe that your talent and hard work are enough to assure you a successful career, this book is also for you, because you are on a dangerous path covered with political land mines!

Everything I learned about how to navigate the realities of the workplace and get promoted is included in my Political Toolkit, which I'll share with you in this book. These tools helped take me from an entry-level position to running a national company, and they have helped hundreds of women get promoted in competitive male-dominated industries. So if you are serious about your ambition and ready to do the work, you will find in these pages a proven process to get ahead and stay ahead.

The tools provided here will show you a painless path to navigating the workplace effectively so that you can achieve the career of your dreams. So, let's begin!

1

Politics in the Workplace

How It Works and How Women Fit into It

Sallie Krawcheck, once named the most powerful woman on Wall Street, said it felt like she was fired when a restructuring at Bank of America eliminated her role in 2011. She was asked to join the bank to turn around its Merrill Lynch and U.S. Trust wealth management businesses. What seemed like a perfect role for her turned out to be a blindside. Bank of America was a mixture of several cultures due to acquisitions and leadership changes. Though Sallie attempted to navigate and understand the ever-changing political landscape, she was considered an outsider with few ties to any of the powerful cliques within the bank.

Sallie, based in New York, found it challenging to build relationships and camaraderie with her team and the key stakeholders who were in the corporate headquarters in Charlotte, North Carolina: "It's hard to be part of the inside jokes when you're not there or you aren't having a few minutes swapping stories while grabbing a coffee between meetings. I was never part of the meetings-before-the-meetings, or the meetings-after-the-meeting, or the 'real' meeting; I was just part of the official meeting (which in some companies can be the least important meeting of them all)."[1]

Sallie wasn't in the "in crowd." Not only was she not located at the corporate headquarters, but she was still viewed as an outsider to Bank of America culture. She was not invited to these informal meetings where the real politics play out, where important decisions are made. Despite her attempts to gain access, she was unable to maneuver through the complex politics. Because Sallie was astute, she understood her vulnerability as an outsider. But, like many of us, Sallie also believed that her business results would help to maintain her status and substantiate her value to the bank. "I realized I wasn't part of the 'inner circle.' But I mistakenly believed that if my team delivered strong business results—and, as I repeatedly told the team, if we were the business no one had to worry about—we would be successful. But on the day I left, the business was ahead of budget and gaining share."[2]

Sallie is a great example of a woman who is a top performer and incredibly savvy about workplace politics. Her résumé validates this. She had repeatedly overcome political and cultural barriers in her past to achieve top leadership roles. Yet despite her best efforts to understand and master the politics at Bank of America, she was blindsided. Her job was eliminated. And though she was offered another position at a lower level, Sallie decided to leave the bank. She was trumped by the politics.

Derailed in New York City

Cathie Black, a former chair and president of Hearst Magazines, was appointed chancellor of New York City schools by Mayor Bloomberg in November 2010. Mayor Bloomberg believed Cathie was the right candidate based on her extensive management experience. But it was apparent rather quickly that public opinion was against her. After just a few months in the job, a NY1/Marist poll revealed that just 17 percent of New Yorkers approved of her job performance.[3]

Cathie had an incredible track record. She navigated to the top in the publishing world, where women executives were a rare commodity. Despite her obvious success and savvy, however, New Yorkers viewed her from the outset as an outsider to public education and therefore incapable of doing the job. They looked for every opportunity to emphasize her weaknesses and never gave her a chance to prove herself. What looked like a new challenge and opportunity for Cathie turned out to be a blindside. In April 2011, she was forced to step down. Cathie fell victim to the politics and the power of public opinion. The politics derailed her.

What lesson can we learn from Sallie Krawcheck and Cathie Black's experiences? Here are two extremely competent and prominent female executives who were able to reach leadership positions because of their talent, hard work, and political savvy. Yet in each of these situations, they were blindsided and unable to overcome the strong political barriers. This clearly demonstrates the necessity for all of us to understand the political landscape and identify potential land mines.

Every organization has unique political dynamics. In fact, each team within a business line or function often has a different language, different success metrics, and behavioral norms. You have to be willing and capable of adapting not only to get ahead but also to stay ahead.

Politics can make or break your career. This is especially important for women to understand. To our detriment, we continue to avoid workplace politics and set ourselves up to be blindsided and passed over for promotions.

You must ask yourself where you would be today if you had been more politically savvy and tuned in to the way decisions are made in your company. Most important, what is possible for you in the future if you are willing to learn how to effectively navigate the realities of the workplace? What is possible if you are given the tools to master the politics?

For decades, women's advancement in the workplace has been the focus of research and conversation. Unfortunately, we can only point to limited success in this area. Women are inching their way up to leadership positions, but their progress has been very slow. Currently, women hold only 5.2 percent of Fortune 500 CEO positions and 5.4 percent of Fortune 1,000 CEO positions.[4]

Are we frustrated yet? You bet!

We are certainly well prepared and well educated. Women now hold 57 percent of all bachelor's degrees and 51 percent of all doctorates. We now earn 47 percent of law degrees and 45 percent of all master's degrees in business. We enter the workforce with optimism and ambition, and then our goals for career advancement are not realized.

Many theories explain our lack of progress, but the bottom line is that the optimal way for women to circumvent obstacles is through political savvy and relationships. The culture and politics in our organizations still make women's ascent to top positions extremely difficult. Sometimes the politics is so powerful and overwhelming that even superstars like Sallie Krawcheck and Cathie Black cannot survive. For women, the politics is often complicated by gender bias. This was certainly true decades ago when we faced overt discrimination.

For instance, Elizabeth, an executive in the bio/pharma industry, told me her story about her first job out of college. She was one of the few women working in a company that made flavor and fragrance materials. Three weeks into the job, one of the salesmen came into the lab with a request. Elizabeth quickly volunteered that she could make that happen. The man replied, "No, you can't. You're a woman."

Elizabeth said she was shocked at the time and will never forget this incident. She said to herself, "Wow. I thought I could do anything and then I realized there are other people who aren't going to let me do everything because I'm a woman."

Timi Hallem, a partner at Manatt, Phelps & Phillips, LLP, tells her story of gender discrimination early in her career as an attorney: "I had a 3-year-old and a 10-month-old. The managing partner of the firm came into my office and told me that the firm was going to reduce my salary because I was less valuable now that I had children. Because I had young children, there were things that the people who worked with me would not ask me to do, and therefore, that made me less valuable to the firm. I asked whether I'd ever turned anything down or refused to do anything, and was told that it was not the issue—that, no, I had not but that there were things they wouldn't ask me to do—and that in and of itself made me less valuable. So my pay was reduced, and I thought about leaving. I actually interviewed elsewhere, and then I decided that that would, basically, give them too much satisfaction. I decided to first work on building up my practice to the point where they'd be really sorry when I left. Instead, within six months, they restored my pay and gave me back what they had taken away, and decided I didn't deserve to have my pay cut since the clients were clearly happy with me."

For those of you who have recently entered the workforce, I'm sure these stories are shocking. We rarely see examples of discrimination this overt any longer. Now we have the law on our side—it is no longer legal or politically correct to discriminate against women based on their gender—but this has forced gender bias to go underground. Second-generation bias, as it is commonly called, is more challenging because it is subtle, and women are blindsided by it every day.

The point is that you never want to be caught off guard by this. Political savvy helps you to understand which people in your organization support you and support the advancement of women. These are the people you need to build relationships with. Political savvy also helps you to uncover those who are less likely to help you because you are a woman. This is not always easy because these people may justify their behavior based on other reasons, but with keen observation skills and focus, you can learn who pays lip service to the promotion of women and who doesn't. Bottom line: You need to figure out who are your allies and who are your foes.

Lisa, one of my clients and a senior executive in the banking industry, tells me that the old boys' club still exists in banking and these informal networks are difficult for women to access: "Twenty years ago, men were pretty overt about the fact that they didn't really care to make an effort to include women in their inner circle. I think, at this point, it's less overt, but it still exists. And there are different reasons. I think there's definitely an element of men feeling like, if they say the wrong thing or do the wrong thing, they're going to get sued for harassment. So, they need to keep their guard up."

"Sometimes I think there's a 'women versus men' type of thing, just in terms of the kind of things that men will do together—and they won't invite women. Not even for drinks."

Lisa tells the story of how a senior manager at the bank with whom she had a great relationship did not invite her on an all-day fishing trip, yet invited all her male counterparts. Lisa had lunch with him a couple of weeks later and asked him, "If you knew I liked to fish, would you have invited me?" And he said, "Probably not."

She says, "It was a man who I respected, who I knew liked me very much—and who was very much a straitlaced guy, and there was never any question that he treated men and women equally. But then, there's the off-campus event, and he didn't invite me. It's these types of events where people let their guard down. That's where people talk about things that you may not talk about in a formal meeting. And that's where you build relationships. To be excluded from that because you're a woman excludes you from those important conversations."

To Lisa's point, she may never get invited on fishing trips with her male colleagues. She may never be asked to go to Monday night football events because she's a woman. You may have had similar experiences. It is still important to find opportunities to connect and build relationships with these men so they can get to know you beyond your work and your presence in formal meetings. Stay tuned, because access to these informal networks is achievable with political savvy. It is possible to create bonds with the men in these networks even if they don't include you in their activities after work. You have to be creative and make it happen!

Another thing I've learned listening to women is that they understand the importance of "leaning in" and asking for what they want and need, but when they assert themselves, it can backfire because some men are threatened by their assertiveness.

Lori relates her current challenge with "leaning in" at her company: "The higher you get in an organization, the older the men are that you're dealing with, and the less receptive they are to assertive females. I surprise men when I am assertive. And it disturbs them at some very basic level. And those are the folks who are my audience. They're who I need to persuade, and who I need to have some confidence in my capabilities and my leadership. And if I strike them personally on a level that makes them uncomfortable, it puts me automatically behind the eight ball. Their basic understanding of female behavior is challenged. I'm looking for collaboration and some equal footing— something they would gladly give somebody my age who was a man with a family and demographic that they have."

Do you get a similar reaction from men when you speak up or offer a different opinion? Isn't it worth your while to know who would be most receptive to your ideas and the optimal way to communicate with them to avoid land mines? That requires political savvy!

Unconscious bias rears its ugly head in other ways as well. Bias shows up in the stereotypes men and women have relative to work and leadership. For example, I hear from women that they are no longer considered ambitious once they have children. They are frequently passed over for positions that require more travel. We can experience this type of bias from both men and women who hold beliefs that women who are mothers should behave in a certain fashion. And of course, we still earn less money than our male counterparts.

Here's Elizabeth's story: "When I was pregnant with my first son, the woman who had hired me had been appointed to a new job as an individual contributor and another woman came in to take over the group. This woman decided who got the really high-level corporate assignments. Well, I saw these assignments going to other folks. So, I made an appointment with her, and when I walked into her office, I said, 'Arden, can you help me understand why I'm not getting any of these opportunities?' And she did actually say to me, 'Well, I didn't know how willing you were to travel.' And I said, 'But you never asked me. You made that assumption for me.' You could see that she just never considered that I would want to travel, and it was a really good opportunity. She did end up being very open about giving everybody opportunity. I could see how it changed her approach. She stopped making assumptions about what people would say."

In this situation, Elizabeth confronted the woman and asked her directly why she wasn't getting the same high-profile assignments others were offered. If she had not asked the question, she never would have known the reason why she was repeatedly passed over.

There are people in your organization that make assumptions about you because you're a woman. It is not always obvious why we are not given the same opportunities as others. It's critical, therefore, to clearly communicate your goals to your boss and other decision makers who have influence over your career.

How you position yourself in the company with key stakeholders is critical to overcoming this bias. Learning how to effectively articulate your career aspirations and your achievements is an important aspect of political savvy. Identifying the people who would benefit from this information is another critical component.

Another challenge women face is a lack of confidence. Do you wake up at 3 AM in a sweat because you're wondering if you have what it takes to succeed, if others will discover you really aren't that smart? Our internal demons can hold us back. Many women tell me that they believe they aren't good enough to make it and that it is pure luck that they have achieved any success. Their self-doubt prevents them from speaking up and giving their opinions, from asking for more compensation and responsibility. I hear from these women that because they have a need to be liked and please others, they take on too much work and don't delegate. As a consequence, they are not perceived as having leadership potential in an environment that rewards visibility and credibility.

Lack of confidence holds many women back from engaging in politics and leaning in. What I have come to realize through my coaching practice and discussions with women is that many of us don't understand our contribution to business outcomes. We don't recognize our value. Identifying your value proposition is the necessary first step to understanding and believing in your contribution to the company. It inspires your confidence to put forth your ideas and ask for what you deserve. It fuels your ability to build relationships of trust and influence by offering to help others based on your value proposition. These relationships assist you in navigating the workplace by giving you important information about its politics and by promoting you for new opportunities.

In this book, you will learn the significance of self-promotion as both a leadership skill and a political tool. You will learn savvy ways to communicate what you and your team have accomplished and how to sell your ideas across the organization to build political influence.

I'm sure you can relate to some or perhaps all of these examples of barriers to women's advancement. You live with this every day! And yes, we can look internally (our own limiting beliefs), externally (unconscious bias and gender inequality), and every which way to explain the lack of women's progress. Women are still viewed and judged differently than men in the workplace—and this is sometimes subtle and therefore challenging. But political savvy is understanding the culture, whatever it is, and then learning how to best position yourself, given the reality. You cannot ignore the politics any longer if you want to advance your career. Political savvy helps you successfully circumvent the land mines and position yourself for success. Gender bias is just one obstacle you must be aware of when navigating through the workplace.

You deserve to move up.

If you are working really hard and want to get ahead, you certainly don't want to be passed over or pushed aside, right? Well, then, let this be a wake-up call for you. You need to get "real" when it comes to how you fit into the current culture of your organization. You need to take a good hard look at whether or not you have the political savvy to thrive in such an environment, because the reality is that workplace politics can make or break your career!

The reality is that if you have any aspirations for advancement, you cannot afford to ignore the politics. Yes, hard work is important. Yes, performance is important. That being said, once you reach a certain level of technical competence, politics is what makes the difference for your career success.

Right about now, you're probably asking yourself, "Whatever happened to meritocracy? Why can't I get a promotion based on my track record?" Look around your workplace. Is this what's really happening, or are you wishing for a pipe dream? Who is getting promoted? Is their advancement based solely on their performance or on other factors, such as the relationships they have formed and their influence with key people?

For those of you who focus all your efforts on doing good work, you are not alone. Women spend all their time and energy doing their work and getting great results. We do not see the importance of spending time to network with others and build key relationships. As a result, we do not have access to the privileged information about "the rules of the game" that we need to navigate the workplace successfully. We do not have access to the influential networks where key decisions are made. We rely on the traditional methods of receiving information. Most of the time, we get this information too late to be able to use it to our benefit.

For instance, we wait patiently until new positions are posted. The reality is that many times these jobs have already been promised to others and the company is simply going through the motions of interviewing candidates. Has this happened to you?

It happened to Shereen. "I had two interview opportunities in my company for the same position, and I was blindsided. I was highly qualified for the first position for which I posted. I had full support from my direct supervisor, who reached out to others on my behalf. I executed the interview well. I definitely had the background to supersede the other candidate. But then I found out from behind the scenes that the VP went to the Hiring Director and told them to hire the other person because it was her third time interviewing for the job. And so, they went with that person because they were uncomfortable going against the grain, fearing some backlash and knowing that there was a reorganization on the horizon.

"Then I interviewed for the same position a year later, because the girl who got the position quit. There was now a new Hiring Director in place. I was unknown to the new Director. I reposted and again, they went with another candidate, a male, who was very well networked and considered a hot ticket. Everyone knew this person well."

The more we are tapped into the information networks, the greater the likelihood of knowing about new openings before they are formally posted. This knowledge then gives us the advantage of letting others know of our ambition and getting their feedback on how to move forward.

Another example is when we read a job description and believe that we are qualified and meet the requirements for the position. What we don't know is what is involved in the decision-making process: who owes who favors, who will influence these decisions—in other words, the politics. The only information we have is the formal job description. But what will it really take to secure this new position? We're in the dark. That was my blindside experience as well as Shereen's.

Here's the lesson. When you rely on the traditional means of getting information, you miss the boat time and time again. You don't want to appear too pushy or too ambitious and so you continue to wait, living by what you think are the rules of the game. But your refusal to be proactive and political results in you being the last one to know what's really going on.

Do you sometimes feel like an outsider at work? You most likely recognize that there's an "in crowd" that has the ear of senior management. Do you sometimes wonder how to gain access to this exclusive network? And is it worth the effort to do so? You may not want to bother with the politics, but your very survival in the workplace depends on learning who the players are and their unwritten rules.

I'm certain that most of you reading this know only too well that the strength of the old boys' club persists in most organizations. What you may not know is that the best way for you to advance is to gain access to these informal networks by building relationships and using political skill. Politics opens the door to valuable information and shows you the best road map for avoiding land mines and building bridges and allies across the organization. The more expansive your network is, the clearer your path.

You might also be turned off by the notion of "politics" in the workplace. You don't want to get involved. You don't have the time for this. You put in a long day and then rush home to your family. You barely have a life as it is. So how important is this?

It is the knowledge of the workplace systems and culture that gives the politically savvy the advantage. A lack of engagement in politics results in your exclusion from the power networks. You are not connected to the people in the organization who can provide you with information about the way decisions are made and who can influence those decisions.

This lack of engagement in workplace politics by women is often referred to as "political skills deficiency."[5] One can make the argument that this is a viable reason for women's lack of progress. Our lack of engagement in workplace politics not only puts us at a disadvantage or political deficiency, but it also puts us in the "loser's bracket."[6] None of us want to be in the loser's bracket if we have any ambition at all!

Only YOU can answer how important this is for YOU. If you are truly ambitious and want to control your career destiny, then you need to pay attention to the politics. If you sincerely want to move your career forward, this book will be your guide to learning how to be painlessly political.

I understand that engaging in workplace politics is probably not your comfort zone. You would rather focus on your work and not deal with the politics. But what if you had a road map for how to become politically savvy and build the relationships necessary to help you get ahead and stay there?

In this book, you will learn all the tools you need to scope out the political landscape, be strategic, and identify the key relationships you need for your advancement. You will also learn how to build confidence, trust, and influence with these key stakeholders. In short, you will learn how to be politically savvy.

What Is Political Savvy?

Have you ever wondered why some people seem to get a free pass? Their mistakes are minimized and their achievements maximized. Doors open for them, and they enjoy the spotlight without a tremendous amount of fanfare. They may or may not be as competent and talented as you are, but everything they do seems to work in their favor.

These people are politically astute. They have learned how to work the system in a subtle way. They have gained favor with those in power, and this is not by accident. This is a skill. The fact that they have achieved this status without being viewed as manipulative and self-promoting only confirms their skill.

Politically savvy people develop a sense of intuition that helps them to circumvent potential land mines. They observe the environment and take note of what is rewarded and what is disregarded. They observe how people succeed and what is important to the people in power. This observation is critical to developing political skill.

How well are you tuned in to how decisions are made in your organization? These decisions are often not as straightforward as you might think, and the people with power and influence are not necessarily those you see in the upper rankings of the traditional organizational chart.

How strong are your relationships with key stakeholders and influencers? Politically savvy people not only have identified the power brokers but also have developed relationships to increase their visibility and influence.

How do you become politically savvy? You need to observe, listen, and ask questions such as:

Who is getting promoted and why?
With whom do they have relationships?

How are people rewarded in your organization?
What did they do to get noticed?
What types of behavior are not rewarded?
Who can be your champion?
Who seems to be in "favor" and why?
Are there certain people who have access to the leadership team?

In her book, *It's All Politics*, author Kathleen Reardon addresses the importance of observing the environment and learning about potential danger. She mentions primatologist Frans de Waal's studies with chimpanzees. Chimpanzees don't make uncalculated moves. They are great at observing the social landscape. "They are always keeping track of each other, always thinking about the next social step. Three chimps form coalitions and work together to assess their surroundings and deal with potential enemies."[7]

So it seems that even chimps are politically savvy to some degree! This awareness of their environment and willingness to work together contributes to their very survival.

We also need to develop a radar system to understand potential roadblocks and danger. This radar comes from a keen understanding of the people and culture of the organization. This radar system comes from the knowledge that can only be obtained from the inner circles within the workplace that both influence and make the rules of the game.

Betsy Myers, director of the White House Office for Women's Initiatives and Outreach in the Clinton administration, chief operating officer of Obama's first presidential campaign, and now founding director of the Center for Women and Business at Bentley University, spoke to this point when I interviewed her: "I think you have to be conscious of how you come across. You have to watch for what's going on around you—that you can't just operate; you can't just do your work. There's a bigger picture, and you have to stay conscious of what's going on around you. I think that's the big thing—that there are more pieces to the puzzle. Where do you fit in to the puzzle?"

Betsy suggested that you ask yourself these questions:

1. Who are the stakeholders here that care about the work that I'm doing?
2. What are the relationships that I need to build?
3. What are the relationships that need to be improved or strengthened?

"Part of being politically savvy is saying, "What is it that I'm trying to do? And, when I approach someone whose help or involvement I need, I ask myself how can I help them reach their goals?

"So, part of being politically savvy is being able to sell your initiative and your idea or the reason why you need to be at the table, because you actually are—not just because they like you, or, you know, you're fun, or you're smart, or whatever it is—but that you actually help them further their goals."

Betsy says there are two parts to being politically savvy: "Being conscious of the world around me—who is in my corner, who's not? What relationships do I need to build, to spend more time on? And then, being strategic about how to move the ball forward."

According to executive coach and best-selling author, Dr. Lois P. Frankel, political savvy means understanding the nature of the quid pro quo inherent to every relationship. She advises that to be effective at workplace politics, you must provide others with what they need and want in exchange for what you need and want.

Frankel comments on this: "Early in my career, it was difficult to succeed with workplace politics because the 'old boys club' wasn't hospitable to women and I didn't understand how to crack it. I thought working hard would be the best strategy, but that wasn't true then; it isn't true now. I don't know that the 'old boys club' has changed that much, but I've gotten better at building the kinds of quid pro quo relationships that enable me to achieve my goals."

Timi Hallem speaks of the political savvy necessary for female attorneys: "I think it's crucial for female attorneys, because in addition to the usual office politics that everyone faces, in every organization, whether it's a law office, a corporation, academia, or in fact, real politics, there are minefields no matter where you are. For women attorneys, there are more minefields, because you're also going to be dealing with some people, even in this day and age, who are not supportive about either women attorneys, or women who have kids, or part-time work. And you need to know who they are and how to deal with them."

The Importance of Political Will

Political skill is very important, but it is only one part of the equation. Organizations are political arenas, and to be effective in such arenas, you must have both the political will and political skill.[8]

What is political will? It is the willingness to embrace the politics; to understand how decisions are made and how the culture affects those decisions.

The very first thing you need to do is to get real about what it takes to succeed. Time and time again I have seen talented and deserving women passed over for promotions because they are unwilling to pay attention to the way decisions are made and who has the power and influence over those decisions. Are you one of these women?

What will set you apart from others is having both the technical competence and the commitment to understand the political landscape, and how best to use that information to build relationships that protect and position you going forward. Your deliberate avoidance of workplace politics or your unwillingness to engage in it puts you in a vulnerable position. As with my own blindside experience, without essential information about how judgments are made and who makes and influences them, you can only react once decisions are made. You give up your power and influence to affect the decision-making process.

Our mind-set about workplace politics as negative, manipulative, and evil keeps us from "leaning in" and understanding the reality of what it takes to navigate the workplace. It's important to "lean in," but you need to look out before you lean in and familiarize yourself with the realities of the workplace.

I asked the members of my LinkedIn groups some questions to determine how they felt about politics in the workplace and the people they viewed as political. The first question I asked was, *"What comes to mind when you think about politics in the workplace?"*

Here are some of the responses:

"Within any group there is the unassigned 'leader.' This person may not always do the right thing, or is the best employee, but knows how to 'play the game.' "—Elizabeth

"There is entirely too much political upmanship occurring in most workplaces. The person(s) who engage(s) in these games may not always be right or be the best employee but has learned to work the system to make him/her the center of attention and project the appearance that he or she is the most important employee in the workplace."—Georgette

"Unnecessary waste of time. Losing revenue; limiting execution. There should be a course in politics in the workplace. Not everyone likes to work in a manipulative environment and is wired to play games and present themselves as suck ups, pretending to do a job they cannot!"—Catherine

"The idea of politics in the workplace immediately conjures up a pejorative image of someone who is trying to get ahead based on 'schmoozing' versus merit. We have all worked with that person . . . the one who seems to have no substance yet continues to have more and more influence, making you wonder 'who exactly do they have pictures of doing what?' "—Stefanie

From these responses, it is easy to see that workplace politics and women often don't mix well! You can definitely sense the anger and frustration. They express a very strong sentiment of trickery and manipulation.

Marilyn Tam, who has been CEO of Aveda Corp., president of Reebok Apparel and Retail Group, and vice president of Nike Inc., agrees: "Political savvy has a negative connotation because people seem to think that being politically savvy means that you're somewhat sly. Anytime the topic of workplace politics comes up, there seems to be this perspective that there is personal gain involved and it is trying to get something out of the other person instead of understanding it's about human nature. There seems to be a feeling that if we're politically savvy, we must not be leading with our skill set and knowledge and experience. It's almost like cheating."

Linda Descano, managing director and global head of Content & Social, North America Marketing, Citibank, North America, and president and CEO of Women & Co., affirms Marilyn's point of view: "Office politics doesn't need to be dirty or require that you check your integrity at the door. In fact, your integrity is a tremendous asset in building followership. And, workplace politics doesn't have to be about win-lose competition, but collaborative competition through which you elevate yourself as well as others."

Cheryl, one of my LinkedIn respondents, saw the advantage of politics on one level but also how power and influence was misused on another: "I have seen politics at the micro and macro levels of the company. I have seen leaders use politics successfully to get what they want for the benefit of their team, organization, or the company. It can range from support from upper management to funding and resourcing for a new project or program. Or even acceptance of a new policy that has been rooted deep in the company culture for years. I have also witnessed and been the brunt of negative politics where leaders choose a side and stick to it no matter what the cost just for the sake of keeping their ego intact."

What do you observe in your organization? Can you see positive as well as negative politics going on? You can learn a lot from this observation. Find positive role models who exhibit the qualities you would like to emulate. How do they behave and communicate? How do they build influence and use their power? Let negative politics be a lesson for you as well. What type of behavior do the outright manipulators exhibit that turns everyone off?

The second question I posed to the groups was, *"How do you feel about people who are politically savvy and work the system?"* Some of the responses clearly indicate the point of view that people who work the politics are self-serving:

> "Some people just know how to play the game. It could be an inborn skill, learned skill, birth date, seniority, the cookies, friendship, coffee making, or they just self-manage very well. I just can't stand this type of creature."—Rosanna
>
> "I feel discouraged many times because they often do the least work or sabotage the harmony in the workplace with their constant need to 'be the best' when the bosses are around."—Elizabeth
>
> "It is very discouraging to try to work with the people who make their own rules. They are constantly putting themselves ahead of other employees to make the boss believe that they are number one and, on the side, will do anything necessary to sabotage the work of any coworker that they may take a dislike to."—Georgette

Here are some positive responses. When women view using political savvy for the greater good of the team and the company, they acknowledge that it can be worthwhile and, in fact, beneficial.

> "If you are politically savvy for the best interest of the company and not stomping all over ethics and morals, then perhaps it is acceptable.—Catherine
>
> "Early in my career I was naïve enough to think that as long as you did a great job, politics should not matter. Hah hah! At this point, I actually 'admire' people who are politically savvy and work the system if they also deliver results and realize that it is just a means to an end and support the people who deliver

results as well. Being politically savvy and working the system does NOT mean you do not treat people well along the way and have a positive impact on your firm and those around you. The best 'politicians' I have seen in the workplace are also regarded as some of the best leaders (not managers, leaders) I worked with and remain some of the people I would be willing 'to follow into the fire' any day."—Stefanie

"If their hearts and heads are in the right place, then I think being politically savvy can have its benefits not only for employee morale, but it can take a company forward. When people put others before self, being politically savvy, especially in male-dominated organizations, the benefit can be far and wide. Others who have malicious intent and are politically savvy can wreak havoc on an organization, individuals, and a company's bottom line because their intentions are selfish and not for the greater good. They commit unethical atrocities or treat really great people poorly, and because they can work the system, they get away with it for decades."—Cheryl

The next question I asked was, *"What specifically bothers you about these people?"*

"It amazes me that some individuals can continue to blatantly use their power position to wreak havoc and upper management or peers do nothing about it. Individuals who get caught on the wrong side are too afraid to do anything, and, if they do, it can end up destroying a career. Individuals with such intent truly believe they are above the law and do not see their actions as bad, which is also bothersome. It is interesting to me that politics are everywhere. I see it in small teams who refuse to accept new employees into their inner circle despite huge talent. At a company level where leaders are seen from those below them as a cancer in the organization but those above continue to raise them to higher levels. Our country is a great example of how bad the aftermath can be if the intentions are bad and they go unchecked."—Cheryl

"I seem to always fall for their tricks."

"Everything. They can be very vindictive and seem to have a 'God' complex."

"Not a good use of time."

"I get irate thinking about the number of people with whom I have worked that are more concerned about their own positioning than their impact on the firm or the people with whom they work. The people who are 'political' solely to advance their own cause and are willing to throw anyone around them under the proverbial bus at a moment's notice . . . while good well-intentioned people are unmotivated or even worse lose their jobs just because they have not played the game."

My next question was, *"Do you admire the people who are politically savvy and know how to work the system?"*

"Not in the least. I see this personality as all about self."

"No. Karma is evil—what comes around goes around."

"Definitely not. I am who I am and have a great deal of hard work behind me getting to this point in my life without playing games. (Seems like that was my downfall.)"

"NO—How can you admire anyone that works the system and is disrespectful? My father was a SWAT Team Commander. He put the first SWAT Team together in the early 70s and was praised for his concise training, his efforts, and successful in what it truly means to be tactical. He also taught me to walk through life and behave with grace, dignity, and integrity. How is politically savvy and working the system dignified? Criminals work the system; there is no grace, dignity, or integrity in this."

Here, however, is one different response. This woman recognized what a leader can accomplish with political skill and admired her manager's ability to use this skill well to influence others for the greater good of her team and her organization.

> "I once worked for a manager who was incredible at politics. She could walk into a room of 'good old boys' and completely turn them from against even listening to her to having them believe it was their idea. The great thing about this leader was that she put others before self. She didn't care who got credit for her ideas but that they got support, funded, and moved forward at the delight of her organization. This type of politically savvy leader you can't help but admire."

Do you know someone like this in your organization who has the savvy and skills to influence others? As I mentioned previously, make a note of how they achieve their influence; how they communicate; how they behave; who they have close relationships with. This person can be a great role model for you!

Now, granted this quick survey represents a small sample of professional women, but I also get similar responses when I ask these questions in my live workshops. The overwhelming response about workplace politics is negative. Pay close attention to this! It is this very sentiment that prohibits you from seeing the benefit of working the politics in a positive and constructive manner.

Timi Hallem comments on this from the perspective of a female attorney: "There are some women who are suck-ups. And there are some men who are suck-ups, and that's life, right? I think it was worse when I was starting out in the 80s because my perception then was that the men had grudgingly come to accept women, but the women they liked the best were the most passive, who would do whatever they asked them to do and who never made any trouble, never made any waves. And I was not in that group. So ultimately, I made waves if I couldn't politick my way into what I needed. But people who don't understand office politics are completely short-changing themselves. Because it matters for men and it matters even more in my view for the women. And the refusal to see that is a huge mistake."

The majority of women I've asked about workplace politics view the people who work the system for their benefit as political animals. They are seen as manipulative, self-serving "suck-ups" who waste everyone's time. But the fact of the matter is that these manipulative suck-ups have no savvy at all! Their blatant misuse of relationships for their own benefit is proof that they are not socially astute. Politics can be utilized in a positive manner to help you achieve your goals.

Politically savvy individuals work the system in a subtle manner. They are often behind the scenes building relationships of trust and influence. They are not self-serving. They are using their relationships for the greater good of everyone. This sets them apart from the outright manipulators that give office politics a bad name.

"Politically skilled individuals not only know precisely what to do in different social situations at work: They also know exactly how to do it in a manner that diffuses any potentially manipulative motives."[9]

I also asked my LinkedIn groups, *"Does your organization promote people solely based on performance?"* All of the respondents agreed that this was NOT the case.

This puzzles me. If you know this to be true, that the principles of meritocracy are not always upheld, why would you not seek out the people and information that will positively influence your career? Why would you continue to believe that your work alone will get you ahead? Why would you not embrace the politics to learn how best to navigate and realize your ambition?

Politics is everywhere.

Sure, we sometimes get disgusted by the manipulators in our workplace as well as national and local politicians. Around election time, we are turned off by the candidates' posturing, and we get tired of their commercials and the endless debates. But what we don't see is that politics is ever present in our own lives as well and we use it every day to further our cause or personal goals on some level.

Let's take a look at some examples.

It's a girl's night out. You are meeting five of your good friends for dinner at a local restaurant. Do you notice how you and your friends jockey for position at the table? Who sits next to whom? Who shares information with whom? Maybe you choose to sit next to someone because you have some juicy information or gossip to share that you feel will strengthen your friendship with that person. Perhaps you feel on a subconscious level that your information positions you as someone with personal power by being "in the know." Yes—this is politics!

Now I ask you to observe your child at school or at play. Do you notice how certain children play together and avoid others? Aren't bullies seeking power over others? Do you see how children will try to influence the teacher? Maybe they bring in little gifts to get positive attention. Children are very savvy about getting the teacher's attention by exhibiting either exceptional behavior or outright bad behavior. All of this is politics! Even at a young age, children leverage their power and influence for their personal gain or some goal.

It's human nature and it's politics. We use our power and influence every day with our friends and family.

Why are we surprised that there are politics in the workplace?

Ask yourself the five questions I asked my LinkedIn groups:

1. What comes to mind when I think about politics in the workplace?
2. How do I feel about the people who are politically savvy and work the system?
3. What specifically bothers me about them?
4. Do I admire them? Why or why not?
5. Do I work in an organization that promotes solely on performance?

Do you have political will? Are you willing to see the benefits of positive politics? What is your mind-set? Are you willing to engage? Are you willing to learn how to use politics in a positive manner to help you achieve your career goals?

Be honest in your responses to determine if you have a bias against politics. Here's the reality: If you are ambitious, your avoidance of the politics sabotages your efforts to succeed. If you view politics as evil and therefore ignore it, you are setting yourself up as a victim—a victim of potential land mines and blindsides.

If you have a negative belief about workplace politics, work on shifting your mind-set. This is a critical first step! Politics is a fact of life. It's everywhere. When you accept the reality of politics in the workplace and take the time to identify and shift your attitude, then you are ready to navigate the system and position yourself for advancement. Reframe your attitude. Positive politics is an invaluable tool for you to survive and thrive in the workplace. The consequence of avoiding it is not only a lack of advancement but also the increased probability of being blindsided at some point in your career.

Marilyn Tam offers a great tip on how to shift your mind-set. "I say to women if I told you now that you need to learn this software program or this new device to be good at your work, will you do it? They all say, 'Yes, of course. That's part of my work.' And then I'll say this is also part of your work. So if you shift your thinking about some of these other things (the political skills such as networking, promotion, etc.) as being part of your work, everything shifts."

"Honestly, don't think of it as politics. Think of it as relationships. And when you think of it as relationships, you're not doing something that is bragging or boastful or negative or manipulative. You are doing something that is benefiting everyone in the organization because you are sharing and understanding how we can collectively come together in a way that serves."

Here's the good news! Political savvy is a skill, not a trait, and, therefore, you can learn this. What I've observed in my own corporate experience as well as speaking with hundreds of women is that political savvy is often learned over time and sometimes as the result of a traumatic workplace experience. Many women, including myself, were forced to see the impact of politics when they were blindsided by it. Until this point in time, they were solely focused on their performance. They knew that office politics existed but chose to ignore it. They considered it a waste of time until their very survival depended on it.

Marilyn Tam describes a situation early in her career that prompted her to learn the importance of politics. As a senior leader in the company, Marilyn negotiated a severance package with the COO and CFO for an employee who was leaving the company. He was not leaving under the best terms, but he did resign of his own accord. Marilyn believed the package was fair, and everyone involved was in agreement with the terms. However, she overheard a conversation between the COO and this employee in which the employee asked for more compensation. To her dismay, the COO blamed Marilyn for the terms of the agreement. He told the employee that it would be okay with him to offer a more generous package, but his boss (Marilyn) would never agree to offer more. Marilyn was shocked and blindsided by this. The COO apparently had the need to look like the good guy.

"I was so shocked. I didn't know what to say. Because it was so different from everything I had experienced to that point. And I'd known both of these people for three years. It wasn't a new relationship. So what it brought to mind was, 'I wonder what I really don't know.'"

"Until that point I still was naïve to think that everybody would just do what's right and work together and have the common mission of the company in mind. Then I realized that well, maybe not. Maybe some people want only the highest good for themselves."

"It really made me much more aware of the power and the danger, if you will, of ignoring politics. And that it's really part of human nature. It's part of every human interaction. And it has to be addressed or else it can be very destructive to the whole organization as well as to the people involved. It really brought me into the awareness more and gave me the incentive to truly address that up front: private agendas, public agendas, company agendas, or global agendas."

Political savvy can also be learned over time with the use of keen observation and listening skills. A mentor or coach can help you to develop sensitivity to the culture of the organization before you step on a land mine.

In her research on this topic, Lisa Mainiero interviewed 55 high-profile executive women in the 1980s to determine the role corporate politics played in their career histories. Her article, "On Breaking the Glass Ceiling: The Political Seasoning of Powerful Women Executives," is the result of her interviews about their involvement in workplace politics. Most of the women interviewed felt that "politics" was a dirty word and did not admit to engaging in the politics.

Mainiero stated, "A careful analysis of the career histories of these women, however, showed that they developed a sensitivity to corporate politics that belied their comments. As they recounted key developmental events in their careers, it became clear that not only were these women astute observers of their corporate cultures, but they had an ability to build alliances and partnerships that were unequaled among their peers."[10] In essence, they became politically savvy over time.

My interview with Linda Tarr-Whelan confirmed this. Linda, former U.S. ambassador to the United Nations Commission on the Status of Women during the Clinton administration and deputy assistant to President Jimmy Carter for Women's Concerns in the White House, said, "I believe that relationships are primary and all else is secondary, and thinking of this as 'politics' never really occurred to me."

What is involved in learning to be politically savvy? Using Mainiero's work as a guide, I have identified four stages of development. In each of these stages, I have indicated specific characteristics and milestones that will help you figure out where you are in this process and where you need to go to further your political savvy skills.

Stage 1: Naïve Nancy

Stage 1 I call Naïve Nancy. Observing Nancy in the workplace, you will immediately notice that she's completely focused on her work. In fact, if you want to find her, she is most likely in her cubicle or office.

She's not tuned into or even aware of the politics. Unaware of unwritten "Rules of the Game," she is:

- 100 percent work focused
- Learns through positive/negative experiences

I can recall my own experience in this stage of development. I was interviewing for the CEO position at ServiceMaster and had been out to the corporate office in Downers Grove, Illinois, many times for interviews and psychological testing. I flew out for what was to be my final interview dressed in my "power" red suit. As I was waiting in the Human Resource office for my appointment, a woman sheepishly approached me and whispered to me that we (meaning women) don't wear red here. I knew that ServiceMaster was a very conservative company, but I certainly was unaware of the unwritten rules of etiquette and why red would be considered inappropriate for women to wear. (I actually never got an answer to the "why" on this.) The fact is there was an unwritten rule that I had no knowledge of, and I broke the rule because of that lack of information.

You can be in Stage 1 at the very beginning of your career or when you transition to a new role or company and need to learn the rules of the game all over again. Then something occurs that throws you off guard and opens your eyes to the culture and decision-making process. At this point, you begin to move toward Stage 2.

Stage 2: Great Work Greta

- Building a reputation for great performance
- Aware of who has the power and influence in the organization
- Understands the importance of relationships
- Focused on career advancement but does not yet have a plan to move forward
- Limited networking

In this stage, Great Work Greta sees the importance of developing her personal brand and creating visibility and credibility across the organization. She still works very hard but now sees that relationships are also important for her advancement. However, she is not actively building relationships for her career or prioritizing this. She is also aware of the politics but does not yet engage. Greta recognizes that if she wants to get ahead, she needs to focus on her career, not just her work. She has yet to figure out how to fit this into her work schedule.

One of my clients, Katie, who works at a financial services firm managing a digital marketing platform, had a very successful track record yet was trapped in a business unit that had no advancement potential. As she was in Stage 2 of her development, I coached her to better understand her value proposition, and to identify and build a network across the organization so others could easily see her competence and leadership potential. Building these alliances became the focus of her political seasoning and self-promotion efforts. Her efforts transitioned from a laser focus on her work to an outreach to others.

Stage 3: Strategic Sarah

The next stage, Stage 3, is about becoming strategic.

- Learning delegation/management skills
- Building strategic relationships
- Seeking mentors/sponsors/coaches
- Learning to talk about accomplishments

Strategic Sarah is looking at where she wants to go and creating a strategic plan to get there. Her plan includes building relationships with key stakeholders and influencers. Sarah is aware that if she wants to succeed, she needs to delegate to and empower her team and develop her own personal influence and self-promotion skills. In this stage, Sarah first recognizes the importance of working with a coach or finding a mentor and sponsor.

Many of my clients are in this third stage. They have established themselves as talented and hardworking and now realize that they need to work with their team to reach the next level of success. The work involves how to motivate and inspire the team; how to sell their ideas to their supervisors, peers, and direct reports to achieve business outcomes—in other words, how to create influence and be recognized as a talented manager.

One of my clients, Katherine, contacted me to help her create more visibility and credibility for herself in the global financial services firm in which she works. Katherine describes herself as the "go-to person"—the person who gets things done. My interviews with her peers, direct reports, and supervisors confirmed that this was Katherine's reputation in the organization. Though her performance was exemplary, she was perceived as more of a doer than a manager. Coaching her to empower and delegate to her team has improved her executive presence and therefore leadership potential. Helping her to identify and build relationships with the power people resulted in her identifying a sponsor and getting promoted twice in 18 months.

Stage 4: Political Pam

- Using personal influence
- Mentoring others
- Maintaining credibility/visibility
- Leading and inspiring others

In Stage 4, Political Pam has reached a leadership position by leveraging her talent and hard work along with the relationships she has built across the organization. Now at the top of her organization, Pam sees politics as a way of maintaining her status, promoting her ideas, and helping others to move up the ladder. It's more competitive on top, and Pam spends much of her time and energy working the politics. She is a great role model for other women in the company and mentors other men and women to achieve their goals.

My client, Diane, is at this stage. She is COO of a construction company. She worked her way up to senior leadership from an entry-level position. Her responsibilities keep her busy, but she recognizes that she needs to use her personal influence to maintain her status. She hired me as her coach to strengthen her relationship with the CEO and the other members of the leadership team. She offers to mentor others, and she focuses much of her attention on her relationships, especially with the CEO. The coaching has helped her to develop a keen understanding of what he wants and needs, and she leverages this to position herself as an important member of the team and an asset to the company.

Where are you in terms of your political seasoning?

What stage best represents where you are right now (see Figure 1.1)? What do you need to do to move to the next stage of political savvy? Bear in mind, this is always in a state of flux. With a reorganization or new position, you might be thrown back to Stage 1 temporarily until you learn the new rules of the game.

STAGE 1: Naïve Nancy
- ✓ Unaware of the unwritten rules of the game
- ✓ 100% work focused
- ✓ Learn through positive/negative experiences

STAGE 2: Great Work Greta
- ✓ Reputation as competent
- ✓ Importance of relationships
- ✓ Focused on career advancement; no plan to move forward
- ✓ Limited networking

STAGE 3: Strategic Sarah
- ✓ Delegation/management skills
- ✓ Strategic relationships
- ✓ Seeking mentors/sponsors/coach
- ✓ Talking about accomplishments

STAGE 4: Political Pam
- ✓ Using personal influence
- ✓ Mentoring others
- ✓ Maintaining credibility/visibility
- ✓ Lead and inspire others

FIGURE 1.1 The Four Stages of Political Savvy

Your Political Skill

The willingness to accept the importance of workplace politics for your career advancement opens the door for you to learn how best to navigate the political landscape. It prepares you to learn the political skill necessary to thrive in your organization.

There is a common misconception that politically astute people are born that way; that they have the innate talent to understand what motivates and interests others and can modify their behavior accordingly. I do believe that some people are more tuned into their environment and the needs and desires of others by nature, but this is a skill that can be practiced and learned.

Political skill is a matter of focus and intention. You can learn to pay attention to your environment. You can learn to be more sensitive to what it is that people are really saying; to become more aware of what their body language reveals about their thoughts and feelings.

Because it is a skill, not a trait, it can be learned. Can you learn this? YES!

"Political skill is an interpersonal style that combines social astuteness and the ability to execute appropriate behaviors in an engaging manner that inspires confidence, trust, and genuineness."[11]

How would you rate your own political skill?

The *Political Skills Assessment* in Figure 1.2 will help you to measure your own political skill. There are 15 questions that represent three different categories: strategic networking, promotion, and political savvy.

Answer all the questions and use these guidelines to rate yourself based on what best describes you:

1. Never or almost never true
2. Seldom true
3. Sometimes true
4. Often true
5. Almost always true

		Never or almost never true	Seldom true	Sometimes true	Often true	Almost always true
1.	I spend dedicated time at work each week networking with others.	1	2	3	4	5
2.	I know my value proposition and can comfortably talk about my accomplishments.	1	2	3	4	5
3.	I understand the way decisions are made in my organization.	1	2	3	4	5
4.	I network to build allies and champions across the organization.	1	2	3	4	5
5.	I have a good rapport with most people.	1	2	3	4	5
6.	I communicate effectively with people at all levels of the organization.	1	2	3	4	5
7.	I have strong relationships with decision makers and influencers in the organization.	1	2	3	4	5
8.	I have identified my power network: who I know and who I need to know to achieve my goals.	1	2	3	4	5
9.	I call on my network contacts to help me get things done and open doors for my advancement.	1	2	3	4	5
10.	I am well known across the organization as a top performer.	1	2	3	4	5
11.	I have or have identified a potential mentor/sponsor.	1	2	3	4	5
12.	I readily promote the accomplishments of my team.	1	2	3	4	5
13.	I pay close attention to what type of behavior and communication is rewarded.	1	2	3	4	5
14.	I have communicated my career aspirations to my boss and my network.	1	2	3	4	5
15.	I am tuned into the motivations and intentions of others.	1	2	3	4	5

FIGURE 1.2 Political Skills Assessment

Assessment Scorecard

Category 1: Strategic Networking		Category 2: Promotion/Personal Influence		Category 3: Political Savvy	
Questions	Score	Questions	Score	Questions	Score
1.	_____	2.	_____	3.	_____
4.	_____	5.	_____	6.	_____
7.	_____	10.	_____	8.	_____
9.	_____	12.	_____	13.	_____
11.	_____	14.	_____	15.	_____
Total:	_____	Total:	_____	Total:	_____

FIGURE 1.3 Assessment Scorecard

Once you complete all the questions, add up your score in Figure 1.3 for each of the three categories.

Scoring Guidelines

A high level of competence in a category would be 20 to 25.

A medium level of competence would be 15 to 19, and a low level would be below 15.

What have you discovered about yourself? Any surprises?

Strategic Networking

If you scored high in strategic networking, you are well on your way to moving your career forward. You have identified the key stakeholders and influencers, and you are actively networking.

A moderate level of competency in this area might indicate a lack of understanding of who holds the power and influence over your career or a lack of commitment to reach out to these contacts.

A low score in networking most likely means you are still focused on doing the work and not paying attention to the relationship skills you need to succeed.

Self-Promotion/Personal Influence

If you scored high in this category, you understand your value proposition and are actively and intentionally promoting yourself and your team across the organization. You have a great reputation for solid performance. You are good at establishing rapport and building relationships of trust and using your personal influence.

A moderately high score might indicate the need for you to better understand how you contribute to the organization. It might also be reflective of your hesitancy to talk about your achievements.

A low score in this area means that you are most likely too focused on doing the work and believe that your work will speak for itself.

Political Savvy

A high score in this category means you are tuned into the way decisions are made and who holds the power and influence. You are actively building relationships of allies and champions and possible mentors/sponsors.

A moderate score in this area means that you are probably aware of the politics but are not actively engaged; not tuned into what motivates and interests other people. You are cognizant of how certain behaviors are rewarded.

A low score indicates a lack of awareness and engagement. There is a high probability of being blindsided by the politics.

In This Chapter, We Have Learned

- The importance of understanding the politics of your organization to avoid any blindsides.
- The necessity of reframing your negative view of politics and embracing positive politics as a critical part of your career development.

- The four stages of political seasoning that help you identify where you are in the process and where you need to go to move your career forward.
- An assessment of your current political skill, with special attention to self-promotion, strategic networking, and political savvy.

The Political Toolkit: Your Secret Weapon to Compete in a Political Environment

To help women become more politically savvy, I've created the *Political Toolkit*. In the next chapters, you will learn each tool in the process. Mastering these tools will help you successfully navigate the politics in your organization and move your career forward.

The four stages of political seasoning demonstrate that political skills mature over time. We have also seen from the results of our Political Skills Assessment that some of our skills are stronger than others. The goal is to strengthen all your skills by using the tools in the Political Toolkit and to consistently use them to engage in positive office politics and avoid potential blindsides.

Here Are the Tools You Need in Your Political Toolkit

The first tool you need is a *Mirror*. A Mirror? How is that a political tool, you ask? You are going to learn how to use the Mirror for self-reflection in order to identify your value proposition. Chapter 2 describes how your value proposition is the unique way you do the work that contributes to successful business outcomes. Understanding your contribution is the foundation of savvy self-promotion. And authentic self-promotion is a necessary ingredient for political savvy. Articulating your value proposition to your network in subtle and effective ways is one of the most powerful ways to gain visibility and credibility.

The second tool in the Political Toolkit is a *Magnifying Glass*. In Chapter 3, we're going to use the Magnifying Glass to look carefully at your work environment and observe the dynamics. The Magnifying Glass assists you in developing the keen observation skills and focus necessary to understand the politics. It helps you to see beyond the organizational chart to determine who really has power and influence. This important tool helps you to figure out what people want and need in order to gain influence and build trusting relationships. The Magnifying Glass also gives you information about your company culture and any hidden rules that may affect your ability to succeed.

The third tool in the Political Toolkit is a *Pass Go and Collect $200 Card*. Remember this from Monopoly? It was to your advantage to fall on this square and get that card because you advanced faster around the board and collected more money. Wouldn't you like the ability to move forward faster and receive more compensation for your career? The Pass Go Card is strategic networking for your career advancement. An expansive and strong network helps you avoid blindsides and positions you for success. No career is built in a vacuum. We need others to help us do our jobs better and to help us navigate successfully in the workplace. You will learn in Chapter 4 how to use this tool to identify the power grid in your organization; who has the power and influence; who are the key stakeholders and decision makers. You will map out your own power network and identify who you know and who you need to know to move up the ladder.

The fourth tool you need is a *Get Out of Jail Free Card*. This is the fastest and most efficient way to get to the top of your organization. The Get Out of Jail Free Card is sponsorship. Sponsors find high-visibility projects for you and pave the way for your path to leadership. They protect you and allow you to take risks. They promote you across the organization and provide introductions to other people with influence. You definitely want this card in your toolbox. How do you get it? In Chapter 5, you will learn how to position yourself to get a sponsor and identify who makes the best sponsor given where you are in your career and where you want to go. You will learn how to ask for sponsorship and clarify expectations for the relationship.

A *GPS* is the last tool in the Political Toolkit. The GPS is executive coaching. Executive coaches advise you how to use the other tools in your toolbox. They help you understand your unique value proposition. They assist you in communicating your value effectively and building strong relationships of trust. The coaching process helps you to identify your power network and look at your career strategically to forge relationships that will aid your professional growth. A coach will also help you identify and overcome any internal barriers and fears you might have that prevent you from reaching your goals. We will discuss in Chapter 6 how to find a coach and how to use one to reach your career goals.

Once you learn how to use these tools, you will have a road map for success. These tools have been used by hundreds of professional women to successfully navigate the realities of the workplace. Now it's your turn!

2

The Mirror

Your Tool for Savvy Self-Promotion

few months ago, I received a phone call from Susan, who was looking for a coach to help her find a job. She had been out of work for 18 months to have a baby and was ready to rejoin the workforce. She wanted some help with interviewing and promoting herself for employment. I said, "Fabulous! I am certain I can help you!" and asked her what she did. There was no response. In fact, there was such a long silence that I actually thought we were disconnected.

Finally, she spoke and said, "This is my problem! I can't talk about myself at all. I can't articulate what I do, let alone tell someone why they should hire me."

Wow! I thought. She has no idea what value she has to offer an organization. She needs help to understand this if she is to be successful landing a new job and navigating the workplace. She was finally able to tell me she was a financial analyst but had nothing more to add.

At first I thought this was an extreme case, and then I realized that most of us do not truly understand what we bring to the table. If we don't understand our own value, how can we possibly articulate it to others? How can we effectively promote ourselves? We get so caught up in "doing" our jobs that we don't realize how what we do benefits our company—in other words, our value proposition.

Self-promotion is an integral part of political savvy. You can't build the relationships you need without it. You can't get the visibility across the organization required to move your career forward if you don't understand your value proposition and can't articulate it to others.

Promoting yourself with political savvy allows you to compete. Promotion is the tool for competition; for gaining access to the networks and information that influences your career advancement. You need to master the art of promotion to get to the top and stay on top, and the Mirror, the first tool in the Political Toolkit, will help you discover your unique value proposition so you can promote yourself effectively.

Think about it. How can you promote yourself if you don't understand your value proposition? How can you communicate your value to others so they get why they should hire you or give you new responsibilities at work if you don't even know your value? How can you build visibility and influence with key stakeholders and decision makers for your advancement? After all, they need to know how your work benefits the organization. How can you do this if you don't get it yourself?

This is where the Mirror comes in. You need to take the time to reflect and do the inner work to understand your unique value so you can promote yourself with confidence. Without doing this important work, you will continue to feel uncomfortable and hesitant when talking about your accomplishments. You will continue to be invisible. You will be vulnerable to the blindside.

The Mirror helps you to see your value proposition: how the unique way you deliver the work contributes to specific business outcomes. It's an important tool in the Political Toolkit because of our tendency to be externally rather than internally focused. We have a fascination with what everyone else is doing. We are constantly distracted by the activities and accomplishments of others and have little, if any, focus on our true gifts and talent.

The Reality of the Workplace

The current business environment is frenetic. People are too busy today to go out of their way to find, recognize, and reward you. The good news is that you can create the visibility and credibility you need to move your career forward. You can control how others perceive you in the work environment. You can learn to communicate to others what value you bring to the table. In short, you can be visible, take credit for your accomplishments, showcase your skills, and build your reputation both inside and outside your company as a subject matter expert.

If you are waiting for someone to promote you, you are wasting valuable time. It is essential to build your reputation across the organization. You need to promote yourself. You need to promote your team.

Research shows us that men are much better at this. They spend on average about 80 percent of their time doing their work and 20 percent of their time letting everyone else know what a good job they've done. You know this, right? You see it every day. And you may roll your eyes and say they are full of themselves, but the fact of the matter is, they are getting promoted faster. They are receiving higher bonuses and compensation. You shouldn't be rolling your eyes; you should be taking notes!

The reality is that people need to know your value proposition. You will continue to miss out on great opportunities if you remain invisible. Yes, you still need to do a great job, but part of your job is also letting others know your accomplishments and those of your team. You must build influence and political capital.

Shereen, who we met in chapter 1, found this out the hard way when the promotion she wanted went to a man who was better at self-promotion. She made a couple of mistakes. She didn't build a relationship with the decision maker, in this case, the hiring director. She didn't let people know that she also had successfully completed the same in-house project the man had done. The big difference was that even though they had both been successful with this project, the key stakeholders knew of the man's accomplishments but had no knowledge of Shereen's. He was considered the hot ticket, and she was invisible—a tough lesson to learn.

Have you had similar experiences? Someone got the job you are more qualified for, or someone stole your ideas because you failed to promote yourself?

Why do women hesitate to promote themselves? Intellectually we understand the importance of promoting ourselves. So why do we hesitate?

In 2011, Catalyst published a study, *The Myth of the Ideal Worker: Does Doing All the Right Things Really Get Women Ahead?*[1] This research supports the importance for women to communicate their value for their career advancement. After following 3,000 high-potential MBA graduates, Catalyst found that doing all the "right things," such as being proactive, requesting high-profile assignments, and asking for promotions and raises, did not significantly help women advance their careers. What Catalyst found to have a positive impact on women's careers was the communication of their achievements. Women who were able to talk about their accomplishments got more promotions and higher compensation, and they were more satisfied with their careers as a result.

This research clearly demonstrates the benefit of promotion for women in the workplace.

We can also learn valuable lessons from female leaders such as Sharon Allen. Sharon served as chairman of the board of Deloitte LLP from 2003 to 2011. Early in her career, as a manager at Deloitte, she was blindsided when she received an announcement that several of her close colleagues were being promoted and she wasn't. She was upset. After all, she was working very hard and had many accomplishments that demonstrated her qualifications for a promotion. After a day or so, she went to talk to her boss. She told him quite pointedly of her surprise at not being promoted given her performance. She then proceeded to outline for him all her achievements. Apparently, he was equally surprised and said he had no idea she had achieved all that.

"You didn't let me know," he told her. This was the very last time Sharon let that happen! From then on, she made it her intention to let everyone know of her achievements.

Here's the great lesson in this story. We believe that our performance speaks for itself and that everyone knows what we do and how we contribute to the success of our department and our company. But guess what? This is a *huge* assumption and one that will set you up to be blindsided. It's your responsibility not only to keep track of everything that you and your team have accomplished but also to let others know about those successes. Otherwise, you remain invisible and lack the credibility to move your career forward.

Intellectually we get it. We're smart. We grasp the importance of communicating our value to others, but emotionally we still have trouble doing it.

What's going on here? There are four basic reasons why women hesitate to promote themselves in the workplace:

1. Our upbringing.
2. The failure to see self-promotion as a leadership skill. (We only see it as self-serving and, therefore, distasteful.)
3. Our fear of potential backlash: the double bind.
4. Our failure to understand the contribution we make to business outcomes (our value proposition).

Our Upbringing

There is no doubt that in the past, girls have received different messages from boys regarding the importance of humility. Somewhere along the line we got the message that we should be quiet about our talent. We should take the back seat and wait to be recognized. This message has affected generations of women now in the workforce. Our upbringing has subconsciously sabotaged us in this regard. It has contributed to our belief that it is wrong to promote ourselves and take credit for our accomplishments. Intellectually, we may understand how important this is, but we can't help thinking that we are bragging. It feels like we are tooting our horn, and we believe no one will like us as a consequence. In other words, our effort to promote ourselves comes with a whole lot of baggage about how distasteful it is. We simply weren't brought up to do this, and we don't know how to do it well.

On the other hand, boys are taught at an early age to compete. They are encouraged to differentiate themselves and play to win. As a consequence, when they enter the workforce, they've had practice and support for competing, so they do it well.

Hopefully, as more girls enter competitive sports, the message will change, and young girls will also be encouraged to compete and take credit for their wins. It is my hope that we will realize how our own upbringing has put us at a disadvantage in this regard and that we will be more conscious of the advice we give our daughters.

The messages we receive growing up fuel our emotional reaction to self-promotion. It is critical to reframe this negative mind-set before we can move on to learn the other tools in the Political Toolkit. Our hesitancy to take credit for our accomplishments results in a loss of power, influence, and political capital in the workplace.

Another contributing factor to our discomfort and hesitancy to promote ourselves is the emphasis we place on winning the affection of others. Our efforts to please everyone shift our focus from what we want and need to what others think and feel about us. We listen and watch intently for cues and signals from our loved ones about who we are and what we should do. Their opinions soon drown out our inner voice. We lose the connection with what makes us truly unique.

How does this happen?

When we are infants, we want our immediate needs met. Everything is about *us*. We want to be fed. We want our diapers changed. We want to be held. We aren't concerned about what others think about us. We don't worry that if we cry too much, we won't get fed or Mommy won't like us. As we get older, however, we become more aware of the people around us who love us and take care of us, and we want to please them.

When I was four years old, I started taking ballet. I loved it! As I entered elementary school, I took lessons three times a week. In my mind, I was a prima ballerina. There was no question. This was who I was and what I wanted to be when I grew up. It was my passion.

When I was six, our family was invited to my cousin's wedding. The reception was in a large ballroom. All 125 guests were seated at tables around the center dance floor. There was a live orchestra. With my ballet shoes in hand, I took it upon myself to go up to the band leader and ask him if he would please tell everyone to sit down so that I could dance. And also, would he mind playing some slow, soft music?

And there I was, center stage, doing what I loved to do—dance!

I wasn't embarrassed. I didn't think I was bragging. I was sharing my love and passion for dance with everyone there. Now, perhaps my parents were a little taken back by my boldness, but I think they were proud. I know for certain my grandmother was ecstatic because she always encouraged me to showcase my talent.

I'm sure at the time, those in the audience thought I was cute and precocious. I was only six after all. They clapped and smiled and complimented me.

Over time, however, this all changed. As I continued to pursue my love of ballet as a teenager, I heard different messages.

"You don't really want to be a ballerina."

"I don't?"

"No. That's no life for you. It's physically abusive. You can't make a decent living dancing."

And here's the message that really stuck: "Besides, you'll never make it as a ballerina. You're not built like a ballerina. You will fail."

The point here is that I started to listen to everyone else's ideas about who I was and what I should do, and I changed to please them. I lost touch with what I wanted and who I was. We grow up in a society where we are pushed and pulled by parents, friends, and teachers who encourage us with mixed messages, telling us to be all sorts of different things. We lose the connection with the inner voice that once was so loud and clear. We no longer know where we belong. We lose the self-awareness we once had.

This level of self-awareness doesn't necessarily come with intelligence or education. But it does come with self-reflection. We need a Mirror to help us see clearly what we bring to the table.

One of my favorite quotes from Steve Jobs is a great reminder to stay connected with your inner voice and innate wisdom: "Your time is limited, so don't waste it living someone else's life. Don't be trapped by dogma, which is living with the results of other people's thinking. Don't let the noise of others' opinions drown out your own inner voice. And most important, have the courage to follow your heart and intuition. They somehow already know what you truly want to become. Everything else is secondary."

Throughout our childhood, we get mixed messages about who we are. This results in a separation from our inner wisdom. Our default behavior is to listen first to others in order to please them. We have no clue, therefore, what we bring to the table because we are so occupied with what everyone else is contributing.

You will learn in this chapter to use the Mirror for the self-reflection you need to discover your value proposition and promote yourself with authenticity.

Our Failure to See Self-Promotion as a Leadership Skill

Despite the fact that most women understand the importance of self-promotion for their advancement, they do not intentionally use it. We have been conditioned to take the back seat and wait to be recognized. As a consequence, we often have this inner argument about how to proceed with self-promotion. We know we should do more of it. We know we should be better at it. But at the same time, it's much more comfortable to stay focused on doing our work.

We have the mind-set that self-promotion is self-serving and therefore distasteful. Even if we attempt to talk about our accomplishments and take credit for our success, doing this with confidence and conviction is challenging.

It is important to see that self-promotion is a leadership skill. It is your responsibility to talk about what you and your team have achieved, not only for your own benefit, but also for the team and the company. It's how you create influence. It's how you sell your ideas across the organization. It's the basis of building relationships with key stakeholders and gaining access to the power networks.

From this perspective, self-promotion takes on a different purpose. You are letting others know of your accomplishments and your value proposition, and you are offering to help in ways that benefit the organization. Everyone wins. Your team benefits from your promotional efforts. They receive recognition for their efforts and success. You benefit as the team leader who spearheaded the project or initiative, and the company wins as well. The company can use your accomplishments to initiate other projects or ideas across the organization. They can use your success metrics as an example for future endeavors. Without the knowledge about your project, the company cannot leverage your success in other areas.

Self-promotion is not just about you. It's about you, your team, and the organization.

Linda Descano, who we met in Chapter 1, received the Changing the Game Award from Advertising Women of New York in 2013. This award recognized her initiative to change the use of social media at Citi and connect with women. She let her manager know about the award before it went to press. She told him, "While I was the one recognized, this really is a huge win for the entire team." She went on to tell him of a couple of things the team was doing to increase the value this effort was making to the business.

This is savvy self-promotion at its best! It demonstrates how to take credit for your work, give recognition to your team, and show how the initiative benefits the business.

Linda effectively uses self-promotion as a leadership skill. She is a great cheerleader for her team, and her team looks to her to promote their accomplishments across the organization. This year, Linda had the honor of being invited by the global chief marketing officer to make a presentation on social servicing at one of his town hall meetings. Instead of jumping on this opportunity herself, Linda suggested that Paul, one of her team members, do the presentation. "I think the global CMO was sort of taken aback that I didn't just take that opportunity for myself. But Paul was so thrilled that he could step into the spotlight and shine. I find opportunities to give those types of speaking occurrences to my team members. I will give shout outs when someone sends me an unsolicited shout out about someone, and I will copy my boss. I want my folks to be recognized. I want them to be sought out internally for other positions. And I've had a really good track record of folks who work for me being promoted and having great opportunities in other parts of Citi. I don't try to hold them back and pretend that I'm the only one doing the work."

Betsy Myers, former senior advisor to Presidents Clinton and Obama, has always been an advocate for women's issues. She demonstrated promotion as a leadership skill when she aligned her skills and passion for women's issues with President Clinton's reelection campaign. Betsy ran the office for women business owners when she worked for the Small Business Administration (SBA). She recognized that women business owners were a potential Clinton voting bloc. Women had elected him the first time, and they would reelect him. Women voters were thus very important for his reelection.

So Betsy began working her relationships and promoting herself and her ideas for the benefit of President Clinton's reelection: "I started to go over to the White House and meet with different people to say, 'Hey, what can we do to make sure we harness this voting bloc and these women out there? They're the fastest-growing segment of the business economy.'

"I went over there to alert people to what I was doing; the conferences out there where I was speaking that were potential opportunities for the president or someone else to speak at; these statewide conferences on women. And that's where I developed my reputation as someone who was an expert on a particular issue of women entrepreneurs; passionate, supportive of the president and his reelection. And then, when the president decided to create an office in the White House on women's issues, I had made a name for myself and was appointed director of this department."

This was a win for Betsy, for President Clinton, and for women entrepreneurs. This is a great example of using promotion as a leadership skill.

It is possible to use promotion to enhance your credibility by aligning yourself with business initiatives. Demonstrating your leadership and highlighting your team's efforts increases your visibility and benefits your company. Once you are seen as a credible leader, you will have more influence in the organization and can therefore gain access to the informal networks and relationships you need with key stakeholders. You are viewed as someone who adds value to the business. You have political capital.

Sometimes it's just a matter of letting others know what you are accomplishing, as Sharon Allen learned at Deloitte.

How do you do this?

Betsy Myers learned how to strategically inform other stakeholders of her ongoing efforts and successes from her boss, Erskine Bowles. "Erskine Bowles, who was head of the SBA, was really strategic. Every week, he had the chief of staff of the SBA put together a very concrete, simplified version of the contributions he made that week to support the president's goals. It was delivered to the White House, to the chief of staff, deputy chiefs of staff, the president, first lady, and vice president. And within 16 months, Erskine went from being head of the SBA to deputy chief of staff in the White House."

Betsy recalls that initially she thought his weekly memos were manipulative. "But that's how guys do it. The president was trying to get health care done. The president was trying to do these different things, and Erskine was working really hard. And at the time, he wasn't a member of the Cabinet. But later, in the Clinton administration, he became a member of the Cabinet. So, how was he getting information in? How do you do that? How do you let people know? We get so busy and so caught up in what we're doing that we forget to brief the people above us or the people that we're helping."

Betsy's point is well taken. How are you helping? When you tell others what you and your team are accomplishing, you are letting them know how you add value to their project or initiative. You build a reputation as a leader.

Self-promotion is a leadership and political skill that is critical to master in order to navigate the realities of the workplace and position you for success.

Our Fear of Potential Backlash: The Double Bind

Women face a unique conundrum in the workplace. In our culture, a great leader is thought of as someone who is decisive, assertive, and independent. These qualities are most often associated with men. Women, on the other hand, are expected to be nice, nurturing, and unselfish. So what happens when women want to be considered for leadership positions? If we exhibit the assertive qualities associated with the ideal leader, we find ourselves in a "double bind." We may be considered competent and qualified for the position, but we are also viewed as less likeable. We are expected to have more feminine qualities. On the flip side, women in positions of authority who have a more traditional feminine style may be liked, but they are not respected. They are considered too emotional and too soft to be a strong, decisive leader.

For instance, when Lisa worked on a trading floor with male NASDAQ equity traders, she was faced with the double bind when she asserted herself and gave her honest opinion: "They were a very tough crowd. There were many traders and personalities on that floor that had incredibly high opinions of themselves. What I realized is that they liked me only when I was more deferential. And the few times that I dared to challenge one trader with a different opinion he completely shut me out. From that point on, when there were things that he needed done for his desk, he'd go to somebody else and not me. So, it was clear. He basically cut me off, out of his business line."

In this example, Lisa was demonstrating her leadership and expertise. However, it was not well received. Fortunately for Lisa, the senior bosses liked and respected her, and she was able to advance by using her political capital. She had strong upper-level relationships that saved her, and eventually she was moved to another division.

Lisa says she has difficulty promoting herself and managing up: "One time at UBS when I reported to one of the more junior bosses, I had to go to a training course. We had to do these 360-degree feedback evaluations. The feedback I received was that I was over-confident. They didn't use the word 'conceited,' but I almost had this feeling that I was getting this feedback that was saying that I was conceited. And, quite frankly, I've never self-promoted, so I had no idea what I said or did to make that come out. But because that happened, and that happened years ago, I still don't know how to self-promote without putting people off. So, I haven't."

When the reality of the workplace is such that women who behave assertively are not viewed favorably, how do we manage to promote ourselves effectively so that key stakeholders understand our value?

Overcoming the double bind has everything to do with political savvy.

A study done in 2011 at Stanford Graduate School of Business suggests that in the business world, women who are aggressive, assertive, and confident but who can turn these traits on and off, depending on the social circumstances, get more promotions than either men or other women.[2]

Davia Temin, CEO of Temin & Company, states that she interacts more like a man than a woman. She attributes her success to being able to figure out the lay of the land by observing, listening, and trusting her gut, and using assertive communication in a savvy manner. "I'm quite ambitious. I'm straightforward but also fairly humorous, and that gets you through a lot. And I'm somewhat astute and pretty good at positioning things and talking about things in the best light."

How do you know when to turn these masculine traits on and off? How do you know the most effective way to promote yourself in the workplace to gain political capital? Just as the Stanford study and Davia suggest, you do this by observing and learning as much as you can about the people and modifying your behavior and style in a way that will resonate with them. Generic messages are not nearly as effective as those that are customized for your audience based on what you know about them; what they want and need.

You can authentically promote your accomplishments and those of your team by understanding what is important to others and what they want and need. This takes political savvy. It positions you well in the organization as someone with leadership potential.

Failure to Understand Our Contribution to Business Outcomes: Our Value Proposition

We know that our default behavior is to focus 100 percent on our work. We have also learned that our external focus has disconnected us from our inner wisdom and clarity about who we are and our unique gifts and talent.

Our upbringing has sabotaged us by leading us to believe that we should take a back seat and wait to be noticed. For those of you who understand the importance of self-promotion and have attempted to do this and faced some backlash as a result, you have most likely retreated to your cubicle and your comfort zone. The consequence is that the key stakeholders in your organization have no knowledge of what you and your team contribute to the business.

When you understand your value proposition, you can use this to build influence and relationships with key stakeholders. In other words, your value proposition is the foundation of authentic self-promotion, which allows you access to the people in your organization who have the power and control over your career destiny.

Your value proposition is the unique way you deliver the work that contributes to positive business outcomes. The Mirror helps you to see your unique value proposition. Without the use of this tool, you will continue to look at everyone else and miss what is unique about your work, and how it affects others and helps the company reach its goals. That's your power.

Your Unique Value Proposition

Understanding how your work contributes to business outcomes is the key to effective self-promotion. It establishes your credibility with key stakeholders and influencers in the organization. Because we don't often think about how we contribute or what we bring to the table, determining our value proposition can be challenging.

Here is an exercise to help you see your value proposition. First, write down two or three successful situations at work in which you were recently involved. Perhaps you worked on a project or initiative that helped your department exceed their projected revenue goals. Maybe you found a way to increase the productivity of your team that resulted in a decrease in operational costs for your department.

Next, ask yourself what your specific contribution was to the overall success of this situation. If you were on a team, what was your contribution as a team member that moved the project forward, and how did the project benefit the business?

If you were the team leader, how did you keep everyone motivated and focused? How did your leadership impact the success of the project, and how did this impact the business?

Finally, review the first two steps and take some time to internalize this. What does this say about you? How did you contribute to the success? This is your value proposition: how you deliver the work that results in specific business outcomes.

Katie, who we met in Chapter 1, manages a digital marketing platform for a global financial services company. She has a technical background as well as an MBA. When we first started working together, Katie had the goal of increasing her visibility across the organization to move her career forward. Yet she had difficulty understanding her unique value. She couldn't effectively promote herself or build the relationships she needed with decision makers and influencers. Katie knew that her management of this marketing platform resulted in a 34 percent increase in customer loyalty and revenue, but she couldn't show how she directly contributed to these outcomes.

With this value proposition exercise, I coached Katie to understand that she has a unique way of approaching the business. Her business education helps her to see the larger picture of what the requirements are and how best to create success metrics. Her technical expertise provides her with ideas for potential solutions. She is able to use this knowledge to find the right technology to solve problems. She now presents herself across the organization as an expert who can take a business initiative and find the technical solutions that will help the organization achieve their goals. She has the confidence to position herself this way and volunteer for high-profile projects because she understands how she can help others achieve business results. Her connection to her value proposition allows her to present and position herself to help the organization. She is able to articulate how she adds value and improves business outcomes. As a result, Katie's stakeholders and influencers are interested in learning more about how she can help.

How does your value proposition impact the business? Can you align your value proposition to specific business results?

Linda Descano always reminds herself to focus on aligning her value proposition with Citi's business objectives. "How am I helping the brand? How am I raising and delivering value for Citi? Because just as much as Citi has helped me build my brand, my brand also delivers a halo back to Citi." In this way, you can use self-promotion as a political skill to build influence in the organization.

Betsy Myers says that finding out what's important to a person and offering help and solutions is critical. "What is important to this person, and how do I help you do your job? That's how you get everything done. And you know what? I see all the time, even in my own team, people constantly coming in here with problems. And, you know people who keep coming to you with problems that have nothing to do with helping you move your agenda forward. Because there are people who are always putting a monkey on your back, they drain you of your energy. But it's powerful if you say, 'Hey, I know you're trying to—your goal is to'—and then offer to help."

You offer to help based on the value you know you can contribute. Betsy learned a lot from her mentor, Erksine Bowles. He basically said, "What I'm trying to accomplish here, as the head of the SBA, after 10 town hall meetings with small businesses, is to increase loans for small business owners, because, during the previous administration, it was pretty bad. And President Clinton cares about small business owners, and my goal, as head of the SBA, is to increase loans.'"

"So, I'm head of the Woman's Office. What do I do? I create a program to increase lending to women, right? Well, that not only is helping my job, it's helping his job. And it's helping the president. So, every time I go in to see Erskine, it wouldn't be, 'Let me tell you who is getting in my way, or who's making me miserable, or can you do this for me?' I would say, 'Look what I'm doing in my job that is helping you in your job. And by the way, can you help me in this way to make this happen, because it's going make us both look good.' That's how I've operated, always."

Self-promotion as a political tool is a two-step process. You use the Mirror to do the inner work to determine your value proposition. Next, you need to figure out how to position your message in a way that resonates with your audience. What do they care about? What motivates and interests them? Once you know this information, you align your value proposition with their goals and let them know how you are willing to help.

What is the best way to find out this information about people so you can position yourself in a favorable manner? Here are two suggestions:

1. Observe them in the workplace. What gets them excited? What upsets them? What type of communication do they prefer? How are they incentivized? What are their career goals? What are their business goals?
2. Don't make assumptions. Ask direct questions to clarify and validate the information you have. Ask colleagues for additional information if needed.

Use the *Positioning Statement* worksheet in Figure 2.1 for each contact to help you position yourself effectively.

Key stakeholder: _____

What are you trying to achieve/get done?: _____

What information do you know?	What do you need to know?

Does this need to be validated?

_____ YES _____ NO

Your positioning statement:

FIGURE 2.1 Positioning Statement Worksheet

First, enter the names of the people with whom you will be having a conversation, along with your desired outcome. Are you looking for a raise? A promotion? More resources?

Next, write down everything you already know about what motivates and interests these people. What are they trying to achieve? What business goals are their priority?

Write down some questions that will help you better understand them. What else do you need to know about what they want and need? This information will help you figure out how you can add value and offer to help based on your value proposition.

And last, review the information you have to determine how you can position yourself to add value and help them reach their goals.

Here's an example from one of my clients on how powerful this exercise is.

Diane is the COO of a construction company. She hired me as a coach to help her strengthen her relationship with John, the CEO. She felt that he didn't understand the value she contributed to the organization.

The first thing we did was determine her value proposition. Detail oriented and highly organized, Diane has a solid understanding of the business and the ability to see what it needs to move forward. She not only provides structure for the company but also adds value by her proactive approach. She clearly sees the necessity for certain initiatives before anyone else realizes the importance. In this manner, she has helped grow the business and create the underlying structure to support its growth.

We did the Positioning Statement exercise to get a better understanding of her CEO, John. And so I asked Diane to tell me about John.

John is a visionary. He is a micromanager. He sits in on every department meeting and needs to know all the details about everything going on in the company.

Diane is focused on the details. At any point in time, she has a firm grasp on what is happening in each department.

(Can you see the obvious alignment here between his needs and her value proposition?)

John needs the details so he doesn't spend all his valuable time micromanaging his staff. Diane can help him by providing him with the information he needs to make business decisions.

I suggested to Diane that she offer to help John by preparing a weekly status report. In this report, she would give him a detailed account of what was happening in each department. She would create the report with her knowledge of the success metrics and what information would be valuable to John.

When Diane offered to help John with this report, it was with a firm understanding of what was important to him. She aligned her value proposition with what he needed to run the business. It was a win-win. The result was amazing. Immediately, her relationship with John changed. He now clearly sees her value to him as COO and to the organization.

This is a very effective way to use self-promotion as a political tool. In this manner, Diane was able to let John know her value proposition and thus solidify her position as COO in the company, as well as build a stronger relationship with the key stakeholder, John.

Think about how you can inform your boss or the decision makers in your company of your accomplishments and the successes of your team. One great way to do this is to prepare a weekly status report like Diane's. If you meet with your boss on a regular basis, this report can serve as the agenda for your meeting. If you work virtually, send this report on a regular basis and schedule calls with your supervisor to go over the contents. Give some thought as to what's important to your boss and design the report to include pertinent and appropriate content.

Who else in your company would benefit from this information? You can use this report to expand your visibility across the organization as well. You need to have a diverse network that includes those who have both power and influence over your career at every level.

One major benefit to this type of status report is that you are promoting your accomplishments. Another benefit is that in order to complete the report, it is necessary for you to keep a record of everything you are doing. So when your performance review comes, you will have all the documentation you need for your self-review!

Connecting the Dots: Going from Me to We

For Diane to have assumed that John knew her value to the company would have been dangerous. Our work does not speak for itself, and believing this sets you up for a blindside. You need to connect the dots for people so they understand how you contribute to the business (see Figure 2.2). Don't leave it up to chance because chances are, they don't get it.

Marilyn Tam, who we met in chapter 1, has experience with many different cultures, and this helps her understand how important it is to appreciate another person's perspective, because, as she says, "a lot of times, we speak to people the way we want to be heard, the way we think life should be. And the other person may not use the same

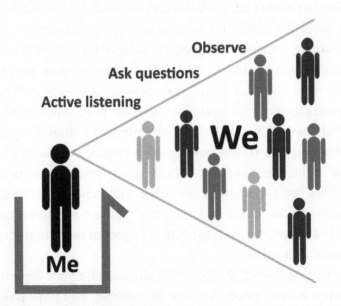

FIGURE 2.2 Think-Outside-Box

words or have the same common understanding. In fact, most of the time, they don't. We need to speak to them from where they are—from where they come from. And having worked in a lot of countries various times in my life—I've worked in up to 120 countries—I understand that every culture, every understanding, and every word means something different to different people. So we have to establish what each word means that is of importance in the mission that we're working collectively on so that we really know what it is that we are expecting from each other."

When Betsy Myers took the position as director of the Center for Women and Business at Bentley University, she made sure that she understood the overall mission of the Center as well as the goals of the university president: "How are you helping the organization that you have chosen? I have chosen to be at Bentley. And so, my job at Bentley is to make this Center the best it can be, because my boss, Gloria Larson, who's the president of the university, made this whole Center happen. This is one of the issues she cares deeply about. It's one of her legacy items. So, my role here is to make sure that Gloria knows what I'm doing to support her initiative and her goals to create this Center, and to move the needle for women in corporate America."

Positioning yourself to help others achieve their goals is powerful. It supports what we know about human nature—that people want to know what's in it for them. You speak their language. When you tailor your conversation to align your value proposition with others' goals and interests, you have their immediate attention. They get how the value you add to the business is a critical component of your political influence. When you help them, you demonstrate your value. They have firsthand experience with how you contribute to the business; your talent and expertise. You are now on their radar screen and positioned well for future opportunities where they may have some influence.

Now you are known across the organization for your expertise, not just your job description. You are memorable. You have positioned yourself as part of the solution. Key stakeholders and influencers understand how what you do adds value because of who you are and your unique talent.

You can also spread the word about your value proposition and accomplishments in collaboration with others. Do you know some like-minded women in your company who are also talented and ambitious? Build relationships with these colleagues and meet with them on a regular basis. It's a great idea to have a common goal to promote each other's achievements across the organization. Make it your monthly agenda to share your successes and agree to talk each other up. Consistently meet each month, share your achievements, and advocate for each other. This is an effective way to promote yourself without tooting your own horn. You promote your colleagues, and they let others know about your accomplishments. You win. Your colleagues benefit from additional exposure as well, and the company wins because it can now leverage the ideas.

Mentors and sponsors help promote you as well, and this can be very powerful. It is also your responsibility to keep them informed of your successes. We will discuss how to leverage these relationships in Chapter 5.

Demonstrate Your Value Proposition

Once you understand your value, what are some of the ways that you can demonstrate your value to others to show your credibility without bragging or proclaiming your greatness?

Here are some suggestions:

- Volunteer to take on high-profile projects at work. Offer to help based on the value you know you can contribute to the project. This gives you the opportunity to show your leadership and ability to work well with a team, and has the additional benefit of giving you more exposure across the company.

  My client, Katie, met with business executives in other departments, asked them if they had any projects that failed or were stalled, and offered her expertise to help them find a technology solution that would rescue the project. In doing so, they quickly learned her value proposition and were able to take advantage of her knowledge and talent. It was a win-win for everyone involved. Katie built her reputation with key stakeholders as a valuable contributor. The executives were able to achieve their goals, and the company met its business objectives.

- Community involvement can be a great way to showcase your abilities while meeting influential people. In the past, I have worked with many organizations that provide resources for women to be successful in business and life. By volunteering my time and expertise with training and marketing, I was able to position myself for a seat on their board of directors.

    What is your passion? Look for organizations in your area of interest. These are excellent opportunities for you to build your subject matter expertise outside of the workplace and expand your network.

    Lisa took advantage of becoming involved in the women's network at work. "Somebody gave me advice a long time ago, and it was at the Women's Network at UBS. And this woman gave some of the best pieces of advice that I ever had. She basically told me, 'You stand in a cocktail party, and nobody knows what you can do. But when you belong to these network clubs, or events, or these formal networks and take a leadership role in those things, you get out in front of people. You organize things.' Through my leadership at the Women's Network, I had exposure to senior leaders in that company that I had never seen before. And through the years, because I built relationships while I was working with people, I was always one of these people that people could come to and ask me for advice, or ask me to help them—even at work. So that, when I called them again, they had a good feeling about me."

- Volunteer to sit on nonprofit boards. This is a great way to showcase your leadership skills and ability to work well with teams to accomplish projects/events and to meet influential people. These people might be in the position to help you by making connections for you and opening doors for future opportunities.

If you are managing a team for the agency, you should include these experiences on your résumé. When asked about your leadership experience, you can refer to this and your ability to manage the team to meet project goals.

- Speak up in meetings and let your opinion be known. Once you understand your value proposition, you realize that your opinion is valuable. You have a lot to offer. Let others know your thoughts and opinions by sharing them openly in meetings. Even if you have a different opinion, if it is presented well and based on sound facts, you will gain the respect of your colleagues, which demonstrates your value to the organization.

- Take credit for your accomplishments. Don't minimize your success.

  When someone recognizes your work, say, "Thank you. I appreciate you acknowledging the effort that was involved in completing that project." Is that so difficult? Or do you always have to negate the compliment?

  Linda Descano comments on this: "I'm not a huge, extroverted, big loudmouth person; I'm an introvert. I've won like four or five awards this year—and I shared the news. When people congratulate me, I don't act like it was nothing. I say, 'Thank you.' I say, 'I feel really good. I'm really proud of what my team and I have accomplished.' But I don't shy away, like it's not important or I didn't do anything—or it was luck. Because I work darn hard."

- A blog is a great way to showcase your subject matter expertise. Start your own blog or find blogs that have similar interests and offer guest posts.

  Many bloggers have built a large following based on their expertise. Maybe you are a great organizer and can give valuable tips to others on how to improve their time management or declutter their work space. Maybe you have technical skills that can help entrepreneurs or startup companies. The possibilities are endless. Start with your value proposition and go from there.

- Submit articles to publications in your industry or area of expertise.
- Offer to speak at local organizations or industry-related events.
- Teach a local continuing education course. Teach a course at a community college. Perhaps apply for an adjunct professorship. Think about how you can help others with a particular skill based on your value proposition. As an instructor, you build your subject matter expertise and spread the word about your talent. And everyone benefits!
- Seek out radio or TV interviews. There are many radio interview opportunities. Look through the podcast directory for programs that would best showcase your expertise. Reach out to the hosts and offer an interview. You can even take it one step further by transcribing the interview and using it for an article or blog post.[3]

All these suggestions contribute to creating not only visibility but also credibility as you begin to establish yourself as a subject matter expert and demonstrate your value.

The first step is to use the Mirror to understand your unique value proposition. Then you can see clearly how you can add value and help others while promoting your expertise. As you demonstrate your value, you are building political influence.

Once you establish the connection with what makes you successful, how do you stay connected and not get distracted once again by others?

Best-selling author Marci Shimoff was a guest on my radio show a couple of years ago. We were discussing women's relationship with success and the challenges women have articulating their accomplishments. Marci described what she calls the Velcro/Teflon syndrome.

Marci says that we have a stronger connection to our weaknesses than our accomplishments. Our default thinking is to focus on how we didn't measure up; what we should have said or done. In other words, we "should" all over ourselves.

Think about this scenario. You are driving home from work. What do you think about? Chances are you are beating yourself up over something that you failed to do or should have done better, right? How many of you actually spend time after work congratulating yourself on a job well done or giving yourself credit for something you accomplished that day that benefited the company?

I'm certain there aren't too many of you reading this that consistently do the latter. As Marci says, our default behavior is to see ourselves in a negative light. She says this is our "Velcro" thinking. What sticks with us is everything we feel we should have done better.

"Teflon" thinking happens when we receive compliments and recognition for our work, but it doesn't stay with us. Because of our tendency to beat ourselves up and not acknowledge our successes, these compliments roll off us like we were coated in Teflon. They don't stick.

To stay connected with our value proposition, we need to change this up a bit. We need to work on using Velcro to recognize and internalize our contributions.

How do you change your mind-set? Keep a success journal.

At the end of each day, write down everything both big and small that you accomplished that day. Then at the end of the week, review all your entries and reflect on your week. What do all these accomplishments say about you? How do they support your value proposition?

A daily practice of journaling your successes can actually change your brain chemistry. It is possible to create new neural pathways that will reset your default thinking to be positive and self-affirming.

The journal strengthens your connection with your success and helps you to maintain your self-confidence. When you feel good about the value you offer your organization, communicating and demonstrating your value to others is much easier.

In This Chapter, We Have Learned

- How our upbringing has sabotaged our self-promotion efforts.
- The importance of self-promotion as both a leadership and political tool.
- How to use the Mirror to reflect and connect with our value proposition.
- How to use our value proposition to build influence with key stakeholders.

Now that you've learned how to use the Mirror to identify and articulate your value proposition, it's time to master the next tool in the Political Toolkit: the Magnifying Glass.

The Magnifying Glass is useful for focusing on and observing the work environment. It helps you to clearly see the realities of the workplace and assists you in creating a road map to navigate successfully. Onward!

3

The Magnifying Glass

Observing Workplace Dynamics

S ometimes, no matter how hard you're working, things fall
   through the cracks. You're busy doing your job. You think that
you are keeping everyone informed, but suddenly you realize you
were so focused on your work that you didn't see the obvious, and
it can harm your career if you're not careful. This happened to
Betsy Myers.

As director of the newly created White House Office for Women's
Initiatives and Outreach (the Women's Office), Betsy reported to
President Clinton and his staff. There was a set meeting structure and
formal chain of command, so it was understandable that Betsy would
focus her efforts on keeping the president's staff informed of her
progress. She met with his staff every week.

But one day, Evelyn Lieberman, deputy chief of staff and a trusted
colleague of Betsy's, took her aside and told her that the First Lady was
upset. Apparently Hillary was caught off guard because she had not
been informed of some recent activities in the Women's Office. Betsy,
who was so focused on the chain of command, didn't notice the
big-picture workplace dynamics, and in this case she didn't include a
key stakeholder, Mrs. Clinton, in her briefs and communications.
Potentially, it could have been a disaster.

Fortunately, Betsy got a heads-up from Evelyn, her ally, and was able to sit down with the First Lady's team to work it out. Together they made a plan to meet on a regular basis for briefings.

Here's my question for you: What are you missing because you're not looking?

Not looking can result in losing a job, losing out on a promotion, losing credibility, or losing face. The purpose of the Magnifying Glass is to help you stay focused on all the workplace dynamics and how they affect you in your current position or your future career. The Magnifying Glass is one of the most important tools in your Political Toolkit, and you need to use it every day. Your keen observation of the workplace will help you to find allies and champions, align yourself with those who have power and influence, and understand the culture. All this information is critical for you to position yourself for advancement and avoid potential land mines.

How many times has your company reorganized itself? Over the course of my corporate career, I lost count of the number of mergers, acquisitions, and new initiatives that led to significant changes in the organizational structure. With each change, there were shifts in the workplace dynamics. I had a new manager, and there were often a new set of rules I needed to learn in order to survive and thrive.

The dynamics are constantly changing. People come and go. New positions and loyalties are created. Those who have power in the organization may change roles or potentially lose their influence. Perhaps their new role will no longer impact your career. Or maybe they've moved into a position that can now help you advance. What is important to realize is that the power and influence constantly change, and if you keep your head down and don't pay attention to what's happening, you are vulnerable to the power plays and can potentially lose the ability to leverage relationships.

Are you paying attention to what happens when there are changes?

Elizabeth says that several times during her career, new leaders were brought in at the upper level, but her allegiance was with someone whom the senior leaders didn't necessarily like. She was considered part of the old leadership team. "I quickly realized that I could be collateral damage in that realignment. And if your leader ends up getting asked to leave the organization, you're probably next, especially if you and that leader were a tag team, or very close; you're that person's right-hand person."

Rita works for a small investment firm in New York. Hired by one of the senior executives to sell hedge funds, she was positioned for success. She reported directly to him. But things changed. The company reorganized, and the result was another layer of management between Rita and senior leadership. Her new manager, a rock star in terms of bringing revenue into the firm, has no management experience and is not invested in helping Rita build the hedge fund business. Overnight, Rita now finds herself in a situation where she has no support or visibility to senior leaders. The fact that she doesn't get along with her new boss complicates the dynamics even more, and now Rita is struggling to figure out how to survive and thrive in a hostile environment.

You need to stay tuned to what's happening and see the whole picture. Having the Magnifying Glass in your Political Toolkit helps you to see the obvious dynamics as well as what's happening behind the scenes, behind the organizational chart.

Barbara Annis & Associates, in partnership with Thomson Reuters and Women of Influence, Canada, surveyed 326 senior executive women in North America in November 2013 to determine how successful women are advancing today and what their challenges are. Their findings confirmed that "women, even at the pinnacle of their careers, are still challenged in steering through the unwritten policies and procedures, yet they understand that the only way to achieve results is to learn the rules for navigating the system." In fact, 77 percent of the respondents said their challenge was navigating the system "by finding new opportunities and effectively negotiating the chain of command."[1]

You learn the rules of the game by making it your intention to see what's happening. The challenge in maneuvering through the system is that there are often different sets of rules for different people in the organization. There are the stated policies and procedures and then the reality of the way things actually happen. The Magnifying Glass is your tool to observe it all and understand how all of it affects you in your position and your business unit, as well as your potential in the organization. You never want to be in a situation where you are caught off guard because you weren't paying attention. Use the Magnifying Glass every day!

So grab your Magnifying Glass, and let's get started! Be the observer and take notes as you learn the reality of your workplace.

There are three main things you need to look for in your organization: *the Power, the Rules,* and *the Culture.* We're going to use the Magnifying Glass to see not only the company's official position on each of these but also what the reality is.

The Power

It is a common assumption that power is dictated by the organizational chart. Yet it is naïve to assume that the hierarchical structure is the basis of power. Rarely are decisions made by one person alone. You must constantly look to see who influences those in command. Big titles mean more responsibility, direct reports, and compensation, and in many companies, senior management has considerable power. But in reality, how do things get done in your company? How do decisions get made? Understanding this is the key to uncovering the power trail.

Timi Hallem, who we met in Chapter 1, says there are some people who clearly have power via the positions they hold; for example, the managing partner of a law firm or the head of a department. "Those are the obvious ones. It takes a while to figure out the real politics, the people who don't have a position—but whose voice speaks louder than other people's voices. And the only way you figure that out is by watching and listening and trying to see issues and results, and figure out who was the most influential in them, and learn from that experience."

If you follow the decision-making process, you will see not only who has the power and final say but also who influences those decisions. It's of paramount importance for you to understand how this all works relative to your position and your career advancement. In other words, who has the power and influence over decisions that directly or indirectly impact you? Who controls access to resources that can help your performance? Who decides when and how you will be promoted?

Early in her career, Linda Descano took a position with a consulting company in Texas. She did her homework and understood from the onset that her new boss had a reputation as being extremely difficult. Most people did not want to work with him. With this knowledge, she made it her intention to build a great relationship with her boss. Linda studied his habits and behavior and came in early every day because she learned that her boss would drop off any mail for his assistants in the morning, so she would be there to greet him. She stayed late as well because she figured out when he would come and pick up things that he needed to review. It was an excellent time to talk to him.

Linda was extremely successful in building a relationship with her boss. Others commented that they had never seen him so happy. So you can imagine how shocked and upset she was when her first performance review from the COO was terrible! She was totally blindsided. It seemed that 99 percent of the people she worked with hated her. They thought she was a brownnoser.

What Linda failed to do as a newcomer was observe all the workplace dynamics. She focused all her attention on her boss and alienated the rest of the team. She didn't realize that although her boss had influence, the COO had the real power over her career. He was in charge of assessing her performance with input from not only her boss but also the entire department. Her boss and her team were important members of her influential network. Linda's one successful relationship with her boss was not going to save her unless she modified her behavior to be more tuned into the team.

To salvage this situation, Linda remained focused on building a good working relationship with her boss, but she also spent more time socializing with the team. In this manner, she avoided the brownnoser label. It's okay to try to please and gain favor with those in powerful positions, but it's also important to be aware of the need to build a wider network of allies and influencers. When Linda changed her dialogue with the team to be more inclusive, asking others' opinions and acknowledging their contributions, within six months everyone wanted to work with her. From that point on, her performance reviews were stellar.

As I described in the Introduction, in my own career, when I failed to see the big picture and understand the workplace dynamics, I made inaccurate assumptions that resulted in me losing out on a promotion. Like Linda, Betsy, and many other women I have interviewed and coached, the failure is in not observing and understanding the reality of the work environment, and in not understanding that the dynamics can change overnight. Every company and every department is different. In my case, after a reorganization, I did not have the information about how the decision would be made to fill the new vice president slot I was seeking. If I had had that information and if I had been aware of who would influence the decision, I would have been able to better position myself for the promotion.

Who Has the Power and Influence in Your Company?

Betsy Myers's innate curiosity has helped her figure out who has the power. She says she has always been curious about her work environment. "I think that's been helpful for me. Why do people do what they do? Why is it that one cabinet secretary is so powerful?"

Betsy would observe Bob Rubin, Clinton's treasury secretary, as he walked down the halls of the White House, and noticed that people would almost bow in respect. She asked herself, "Would they feel the same about another person? What was it about people who had the respect? And, oftentimes, they had the relationships. They were savvy. They were smart. So I think because I was so curious, I watched that as well."

It often takes this type of curiosity and a continued focus to determine who holds the power and influence.

Mia was brought into an organization to initiate change and create a more collaborative working environment. "My CEO bought into this, but there were others that didn't. In particular, our head of human resources—who once felt that an initiative like that should come from her area—not somebody running sales. And so, almost from day one, it really sullied our relationship—and it created an antagonistic relationship between us, and we've had to work together. But what I realized very early on was that we had a CEO who is incredibly partial to her. So while he could say, 'You know, I don't always agree with what she does,' he never corrected it. And this predates me, actually; it became more obvious when I came, because our styles clashed. And he just wasn't willing to defend my point of view—or to defend me. And, to this point, I'm not quite sure that I understand the relationship between them, but she generates an enormous amount of power from her closeness with him. And it just means that, over time, I've been shut off."

In Mia's case, if you only looked at the organizational chart, you would assume the CEO had the power. He did, however, give up his power to the head of HR. This ultimately led to a very difficult situation for Mia to manage as it became obvious that the CEO was not going to take the control back.

In a situation like this, it is critical to align yourself with the one who has the power and yet be conscious of the motivations and interests of all those in the influence circle. In this case, the CEO was paying lip service to initiating these changes. Mia's attempts to get the CEO to back her up did not help her efforts because he was not willing to confront the HR executive. She was the person whom Mia needed to focus on building a relationship with, despite the challenges created by the issue at hand. Including this woman in Mia's plan and getting her buy-in was paramount to its success. She should

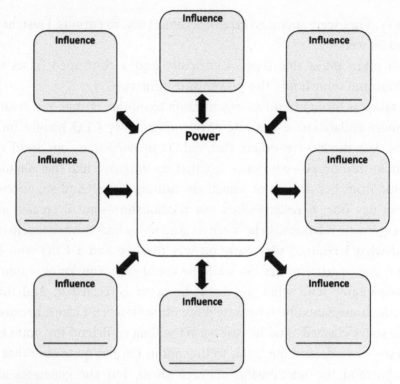

FIGURE 3.1 Power–influence Template

have kept the CEO in the loop but not look to him to solve the problem with the HR person. Mia was eventually shut out and forced out because she could not be effective in her role. She aligned herself with the wrong person: the person one would assume had the power but didn't.

Look at your organizational chart, first for the company and then for your business unit specifically. Identify each person who has direct power over your career advancement. Use the template in Figure 3.1 for each person and put their name in the inner box. If you're unclear, now is the time to use the Magnifying Glass and ask questions. Now identify those people who have influence with this power broker and enter their names in the surrounding boxes. For example, the ultimate decision maker might be a hiring manager. Who does he/she consult with before making a final decision?

In Chapter 4, we will discuss further how to use this information to better navigate the system and build a network that supports your career advancement.

You can also use this template when evaluating any decision-making process in which you are involved. For instance, who is the gatekeeper for resources? That person would be in the Power box in the diagram, and everyone that influences that person would be noted in the surrounding boxes. Assess the situation carefully before you dive in. Who has the power, and who makes the final decisions? Who are the people who influence these decisions? The success of your initiative is based on the strength of your relationship with these people.

When you align yourself with those who have the power and influence, many things begin to change. This was Cara's experience at Disney. She worked in information technology (IT), and her job was to save the company money. "I had to negotiate hundreds of thousands—and soon-to-be millions of dollars—in hardware and software. And I quickly learned that it's very competitive and vendors competed for the business. But they didn't compete with me; they weren't trying to sell me. They would go straight to the CTO. So I quickly realized that there was a conflict going on."

"I would go, and I would do all this research and negotiations and requests for proposals [RFPs]. And I would say, 'This is why we need to spend the $2 million here, rather than $4 million with this vendor.' But if the CTO had a personal relationship with the vendor—or if they gave him tickets, or took him out to lunch, or influenced him in any way—he had the final call. So clearly, there was a conflict going on. And I realized this and started to push back. I had to do quarterly reports, and I ended up having to present them to the CFO of the company. And it became apparent that, really, my position needed to be in Finance—and not in IT—to avoid these conflicts, and the possible appearance of impropriety, or actual impropriety."

"The moment the CFO started making plans for me to go under him, my manager, with whom I had an excellent working relationship, and the guys in IT, the Help Desk guys—who I had an excellent relationship with—all of a sudden, the whole tone changed. Rather than seeing me as someone that they could take advantage of and buy whatever they wanted through me—they realized that that was going to stop."

What Cara witnessed was a power shift that now supported her position to reduce IT costs. Before this shift, everyone bypassed her and went directly to the CTO for approval despite her recommendations. Once the CFO stepped in and asserted his power and influence, the game was over. This move bolstered Cara's own power to be able to do her job. She was now aligned with the power source!

When you have the support of those with power, you get immediate respect in the organization. Another important benefit is that you are now empowered to do great work and are positioned to get recognition for your efforts.

Getting the buy-in from influencers is also helpful in securing support from those in power.

Doris Jean talks about a project she was leading where she needed a lot of staffing support. "My boss at the time, no matter how I came up with the argument, was not approving the additional staff." Doris went to her boss, laid out everything, and he still wasn't budging.

"Meanwhile, I saw that another, much senior manager, was getting staff. And I could tell that she was very experienced using her networking skills to get what she wanted. I said to myself, 'Okay, my boss really wants me to fail. Or he doesn't care about the project.' But deep down, I didn't have the conscience to let things fail by not following through. In the end, I was finally able to resolve the problem by observing how this senior manager built consensus and found out who his influencers were." Aligning the influencers with the project and getting their approval opened the door for Doris Jean to get what she needed. Her boss had to hear from his influencers in order to sign off on the necessary staff.

Who Seems to Be in Favor?

Anne tells me that there are no private offices in her department at the bank. Everyone sits in an open area. The organization of the workspace, however, is indicative of certain dynamics. For instance, her boss sits next to a young woman, and most of the day they are engaged in deep conversation. It is obvious to all the members of the team that they are sharing stories, laughing to the exclusion of everyone else. This woman is in "favor" with the boss. Anne doesn't understand why she has this status, but the reality is clear. Her status gives her influence. She has the ear of management.

When I first started coaching Anne, she was obsessed with how unfair this was. After all, she was doing great work but couldn't get her boss's attention. In this case, I coached Anne to change her focus from that relationship to the one she had with her boss. And I urged her to continue to build and nurture a relationship with him as well as attempt to get to know the "other woman." Though the woman had no interest in becoming close to Anne, Anne's efforts to better understand what motivates her boss have helped her strengthen that bond. She is gaining more knowledge of what's important to him and how to add value. As a result, her relationship with him has vastly improved despite his favoritism because he now sees how Anne can help the business and his career advancement.

When there are obvious allegiances and favoritism in the organization, it may be an indication of deeper, more involved connections, but expanding your network and building your own allies helps protect you.

Use the Magnifying Glass to observe your workplace and notice who sits next to whom in meetings. Who goes to lunch together all the time? Who socializes outside of the office? How does this influence the way decisions are made?

Cara was struggling to understand why a large contract was awarded to a vendor without going through the proper channels of approval.

"I did some digging—like, I'm talking a lot of digging—and I found out that the CEO of the software company—the male VP and this consultant—all lived in the same neighborhood. And then, I found out all their kids are on the same baseball team." That's an "aha" moment for sure!

Cara was in a difficult situation because the CEO had the power to break the rules, and the entire chain of command, including her boss and the consultant, had a strong bond of which she was not initially aware. Very often relationships like these trump the rules. That's the reality, and you need to know what the reality is so you can navigate successfully. In this case, it would not have been politically savvy for Cara to fight for what she felt was right. It would be career sabotage. If she found it too difficult to accept, she would have to look for another position in another company. She had no power behind her to do what she felt was the right thing.

Who Initiates Change in Your Organization?

Understanding this process can help you identify the people who have power and influence. If change starts at the top as it often does in many companies, the CEO and senior executive team have the power and have made the decision to initiate change. Before the decisions were made and/or before implementation begins, did they consult others in the organization? Who are those people? They clearly have influence and the ear of senior management. Who is on the implementation team? These people are trusted and often rewarded for their loyalty and commitment. They also have influence.

If new initiatives are driven from the bottom up, who are the champions of change? These people are powerful influencers who have strong networks across the organization that most likely reach the C suite. When we talk about identifying your power network in the next chapter, you will want to include these people.

The Rules

Most organizations have policies and procedures. If you're not sure what they are, a quick glance at the employee handbook will give you some insight as to the rules and the expectations for behavior and ethics. This handbook provides employees with a road map for navigating the system. It includes policies about vacation, maternity leave, paid time off, travel, and sometimes bonus plans.

When you first start working with a company, you are informed of the rules in your orientation. But almost immediately, you will notice that these may be formal rules for how the company operates, but not everyone follows these rules. In fact, as you become more focused on the reality of your workplace with the help of a Magnifying Glass, you will discover that there are many hidden rules. The challenge is discovering what these hidden rules are so you don't get caught off guard. Often there is a different set of rules for different people in different departments. Perhaps you have been told, "This is the way we do it in this department" when you take a new assignment. Yes, this may not be written in the employee handbook, but this is reality. It's actually a gift if someone tells you the rules! Otherwise you are on your own to discover how things work. Often you uncover this by trial and error when you are on the job, and some of those experiences can be damaging to your career. You definitely want to be as proactive as possible to uncover the hidden rules. If you are uncertain of the rules, ask colleagues and people you trust.

What Are the Hidden Rules in Your Organization?

Julie recognizes that the person who barks the loudest gets what he or she wants in her company. "It is not the quality of the work, unfortunately. And also, it's about not confronting people directly when there's an issue; it's going behind their back, talking to someone else to get what you want, which I've noticed is the case of two people here that wanted to get a promotion. One woman, who is an analyst on the team, went behind the manager's back to the higher-level people who were deciding who does what. And she got the manager kicked out of the team, and she's now the manager of that fund."

In this case, the rules of conduct are ignored for personal gain, and the way to get ahead appears to be through manipulation and power plays. Some people write their own rules and get away with it. In this company, it appears that this behavior is not only tolerated but rewarded. However, if you look closely, you might discover that only certain people get away with this behavior. Are there different rules for different people?

When Cara was given the task of hiring an outside consultant for a project, she was told by the CEO to forget about sending out an RFP, which usually begins the long evaluation and selection process, and to hire the consultant he wanted for an exorbitant fee. She was directed to ignore the formal policies and procedures. The CEO had the power to break the rules.

Why is this all-important? Uncovering the hidden rules helps you avoid the land mines and position yourself for advancement. Observe the way things get done in your organization. Do some people break the rules and get away with it? What allows them to do so? Is it their power and influence? Who has their back?

Use your Magnifying Glass to see all the workplace dynamics related to the rules. Does the organization respect the rules? Are some rules sacred? You certainly don't want to break those rules. You can find yourself in a vulnerable situation immediately.

If not all the rules are sacred, which ones seem to be important and aligned with company values? Which rules are important to your immediate boss? To his/her boss? Be aware of what's important to the key stakeholders and influencers.

Let's examine some of the common formal rules and look under the covers to see the reality.

The Stated Rule: It's a Meritocracy *"We hire and promote the best people for the job."*

What are the hidden rules? If people are not evaluated solely on performance or stated guidelines, then what else counts?

Anisha works at a large global company. She says that in order to get promoted, you have to have done your time. "It doesn't matter how much of a rock star you are; if you haven't been an associate for at least three years—if you've haven't done a brand building and a brand development role—you will not promote, 99.9 percent of the time. You know, if you're a brand manager, and you haven't done x, y, z, you will not become a senior brand manager. So, some of it is paying your time—and paying your dues and all that sort of thing.

"When I was an associate, and I had done a brand building and brand involvement role, I started bringing up the conversations with my boss, that I thought that I was ready to be promoted. Then your name goes on a list that says basically, 'You're eligible now for promotion.' And then you have to wait for a position to be open that you want. If the job is posted internally and they haven't picked someone, you interview for it. And after the interview, you either get the job or you don't. That's how promotions happen."

That's basically the procedure at this company. However, the reality is that many times these job postings are already promised to someone in the organization.

What Anisha realized is that getting promoted has a lot to with what they have heard about you from other people. "There is a culture of, 'Oh hey, yeah, you're a senior leader. You know this person that I just interviewed with. Can you send them a note of endorsement?' There's definitely influence where influence is available. So if someone is posting for a role and they know that the hiring manager knows this other person that they have a relationship with, they will definitely ask that person to endorse them, or even if there's not a relationship: 'My VP will help me get that promotion by sending notes of endorsement' and that sort of thing—even when there isn't necessarily a relationship between those two people. And that is, I'd say, 50 percent of it. The other 50 percent truly is, 'Does this person have the skills that I need for this role? Do they have the right background? And have they had the right experience?'"

What is clear from Anisha's experience is that relationships and political influence matter along with performance. People are often handpicked for promotions despite the official posting and policy. "I've been the type of person that lets my work speak for itself, and I'm realizing more and more that that's just not enough. You could be a superstar—and the higher you go, the more it really is about politics. More often than not, I've seen situations where a very eligible person didn't get promoted—or someone else did get promoted because they were just in the right place at the right time and knew the right people."

How do people get promoted in your company? What's the reality?

If you use your Magnifying Glass to look closely at the people who are getting promoted, what do you see? What do they do to get noticed? With whom do they have relationships? Are they aligned with people with power and influence? Do they have a sponsor? Have they been labeled as high potential and placed in special programs? Are they working with a coach? What is giving them the extra advantage? How much of it is performance versus relationships?

If you want to get ahead, you need to understand what it takes to get there. In most organizations, good performance is important for advancement, but how important? And what other factors are taken into consideration? Often it takes not only relationship building but also an extra effort to get noticed and recognized, such as taking on special projects with high visibility or offering to help others based on the value you bring.

Start with your immediate boss and ask what it will take for you to get promoted. Be as specific as possible about your career goal. People are often willing to help when they understand what you want and need. If your boss is not helpful, who else in the organization can mentor you? Ask for feedback on what skills and experience you need to move to the next level. Don't make assumptions that it's just performance. Ask for suggestions about who you need to know in the organization and if he/she would make introductions for you. We will discuss strategic networking further in Chapter 4.

Meritocracy may be the official rule, but not the reality. Most organizations strive for it, but the hidden rules rule.

The Stated Rule: Equal Opportunity *"There is no discrimination or bias, and every employee regardless of race, gender, ethnicity, and age is treated equally when it comes to both opportunity and compensation."*

This rule is most likely on every corporate website as well as in every employee handbook. This is an important rule because of the legal implications of breaking it. There is great sensitivity to these issues in both the public and private arenas. The number of lawsuits for racial discrimination and gender bias indicates this sensitivity. So the rule is very clear—but what is the reality?

In the *Solutions to Women's Advancement* study cited earlier, the authors recommended that women "recognize the business environment for what it is—designed by men for men more than a century ago. Men are very comfortable with the rules, and are often unaware of how their thoughts and actions can cause women to feel excluded and dismissed."[2]

First, let's look at the organizational chart. How diverse is the management team? I laughed when one attendee at a conference where I was speaking told me recently that the senior executives in her company were "male, pale, and stale." Is that true for your company?

There are many factors to consider when you want to uncover the hidden rules about equality in the workplace. The current reality of the organizational chart may not accurately reflect the diversity goals or commitment of the organization to change. Even if the organization has initiatives in place to change, are they truly committed and invested in the change?

Let's take out the Magnifying Glass to uncover what the reality is for you right now as a woman in your company. Where are the women and women of color?

What to Look For

Are There Women in Senior Executive Roles?

What about on the board? When looking at the organizational chart for this information, you will also want to know if these women were brought in from the outside or promoted from within. This helps you to evaluate your potential as a woman to advance. You want to see if the company is actively building a pipeline of women and investing in their professional development.

Timi Hallem tells the story about a woman attorney in Los Angeles who was with one law firm for many, many years and represented the *Los Angeles Times*. "The firm refused to make her a partner—even though she was doing the majority of the work. So, she left and became a partner at a different law firm—and took all that work with her, and she has been incredibly successful as a First Amendment lawyer. When she got passed over for partner, she could have looked for a new in-house job, or opened her own small law firm—but she decided to go to a new law firm, where she's been incredibly successful."

This is an example of someone who really hit some solid barriers in one firm because the culture was not supportive of women, so she moved to another firm that was more open to having a female partner.

Using the Magnifying Glass to observe if there are female partners and senior executives at a company helps you to determine your own career potential there.

Do These Senior Women Have P&L Responsibility?

Are there gendered roles and career paths? In many instances, women are promoted to senior positions in HR, for instance, but these roles have little power and influence because of their inability to directly impact revenue. If these are the only senior roles that women have in your company, it could be a clue that the company is just paying lip service to advancing women.

If you are interested in leadership roles, you must identify the path to get there. What experience are you lacking? Do you want to

My career goal: _____

What attributes/skills/experience currently contribute to my success?	What attributes/skills/experience do I need to reach my goal?

How can I bridge the gap?

Resources?

Education?

Mentor/sponsor?

Experience? Be specific.

Community work?

Internship?

FIGURE 3.2 Bridging the Gap Worksheet

manage a team but have no experience in this area? Volunteer for projects where you have the potential to take a leadership role. These types of opportunities also exist in the community. Working with community-based organizations can help you to get the experience of managing a team, which you then can refer to on your résumé and when promoting yourself.

What other experience do you need to advance? Use the *Bridging the Gap* worksheet shown in Figure 3.2 to help you identify the gap between where you are now and where you want to go with your career.

Sit down with your boss, mentor, sponsor, or HR representative and brainstorm how you can gain the experience needed, and continue to find allies and champions who understand your value.

You will need P&L experience in order to assume an executive role. Where can you get this experience in your company or in the community? Managing even a small budget is a great way to start.

Once you identify the skills and experience you need, put a plan in place to expand your portfolio.

Do Women in the Company Have Power and Influence? Do they take an active part in operations, strategy, and setting the direction of the company? Lack of female role models can be an obstacle for high-achieving women. You will want to identify those women who have power and influence when building your network and seeking potential mentors and sponsors. Aligning yourself with these women can be an important political move to position you for advancement. You want to know how they have become successful, given the culture of the company, and what advice they might have for you to reach your potential.

Does the Company Invest in Developing Women Leaders? Does the company have a women's initiative? Is it supported by senior leadership? If so, who are the executives that support this? Make a note of who they are, as they can be potential mentors or sponsors and it may be beneficial to include them in your network.

Is there a budget for this? This is where your Magnifying Glass is especially helpful in uncovering the reality. Often women's initiatives are formed but lack financial support or the commitment of leadership. If there is no women's network, make the business case to start one. Get involved and show your leadership potential by organizing the effort and selling it to management. If there is a network, but it is dysfunctional or not effective, get involved and work with the team to create programs that support professional development. This gives you great visibility and helps all women in the organization.

Does the Company Have Programs for High Potentials? These programs are designed with individually customized development action plans, usually supported by mentoring, coaching, and exposure to new experiences in the organization.

These programs are very effective, not only for helping you build social capital in the company, but also because they put you on the fast track for advancement. There are often set expectations and accountability associated with such programs to help support your efforts to succeed.

Research reported in the *Harvard Business Review* "makes clear that high-potential talent lists exist, whether or not companies acknowledge them and whether the process for developing them is formal or informal. Of the companies we studied, 98 percent reported that they purposefully identify high potentials. Especially when resources are constrained, companies *do* place disproportionate attention on developing the people they think will lead their organizations into the future."[3]

How do women get tapped for this program? Often it takes some political influence along with great performance to get into these programs. Find out who has the influence and power to recommend you for these programs. Build relationships with these people. Make sure they understand your value proposition. Ask your boss what it will take to get accepted into this program and work toward that goal, and ask if he or she will endorse you. You can also ask Human Resources for this information.

As with promotions and sponsorship, political influence is critical to get recognized for this opportunity. That's why all the tools in the Political Toolkit are important here. You need the Mirror to identify and then effectively communicate how you contribute value to the organization to gain visibility and credibility. You need the Magnifying Glass to determine those with the power and influence to recommend you, and you will need the Pass Go and Collect $200 Card to build a strategic network of allies and champions.

Does the Company Have Formal Sponsorship Programs? In a sponsor relationship, you are working one on one with a senior executive who is invested in your advancement. Sponsors use their relationship capital to help you navigate the system. They recommend you for promising opportunities or assignments. They connect you to other people in the organization who have power and influence, and they protect you so you can take greater risks.

What is the female representation in these programs? As we will discuss in Chapter 5, sponsorship programs are highly effective for career advancement, and you will want to be in a sponsor program if your company has one. If not, we will discuss later in that chapter how to find your own sponsor.

If your company has such a program, use your Magnifying Glass to determine how people get identified for sponsorship, because many companies have hidden rules. Research conducted in 2009 by the *The Globe and Mail* in conjunction with the Center for Work-Life Policy found that men are 46 percent more likely to get tapped for sponsorship than women.[4] Find out what the qualifications are to be included in this program from your supervisor or HR, and use the Magnifying Glass to uncover who has the power and influence to recommend you. If there are formal rules around acceptance, what are they? Is this the reality of how people get identified for the program? Who has the influence to open the door for you? Identify and include them in your power network.

What Does Your Personal Experience Tell You about What It Takes for a Woman to Succeed in Your Company? Are you treated differently than your male colleagues? Does this vary by department or by supervisor? Is your compensation fair?

Who are the women who have reached leadership positions? What have they done to be rewarded and recognized? With whom do they have relationships? Do they have a sponsor or executive coach?

You can learn a lot from these women about what it takes to be successful in your work environment. Use them as a role model.

When Barbara Annis & Associates asked senior executive women what were the key drivers to becoming successful for *Solutions to Women's Advancement*, they confirmed the importance of mentors and role models. They also mentioned in the study that you can learn a lot from observing the men in your company. But they recommended that you "dispel the notion that the only way to succeed is to act like men. Yes, learn from them and from your conversations so the men you work for and with can better understand and act on your needs, but never relinquish your authenticity."[5]

Observe men in meetings. How receptive are they to high-achieving women? Who are the men in your company who have promoted women? As you build your power network, how can you build relationships with these men? Who are the men who do not have women on their team? Notice all the dynamics and align yourself with the men who are sensitive to the advancement of women and give deserving women in the company a fair shake. Identifying executive men who can mentor or sponsor you is also extremely beneficial in positioning yourself in the company.

The Culture

I love the story about two young fish who encounter an older fish swimming the opposite way. He nods at them and says, "Morning, boys, how's the water?" This prompts one of the younger fish to ask the other, "What the hell is water?"[6]

When you are in and of a culture, as the fish are in the water, it's very difficult to see that culture. Here's where the Magnifying Glass is especially helpful. Try seeing, feeling, and even tasting the water you're in every day the way an outsider (land animal) might experience it.

Basically, the culture is the personality of the group. What's tricky about the culture is, once again, it can vary by department and team. One code of behavior may fly with one boss in one department but not with the boss of another.

When the corporate culture is aligned with your own values, it's much easier to be successful. If you are constantly bucking the system, it depletes your energy and morale. So when you are interviewing in a new company, observe the energy in the office. Supportive work environments usually result in happier, productive employees. When everyone is head down without any interaction, the culture does not condone such behavior. A company like this is not collaborative or team oriented.

Nicole says early in her career she worked for a large bank. It was a nine-to-five work environment. Everyone left promptly at five. No one socialized. They all were on their own in terms of their work, and there was barely a culture at all. Later on, when Nicole moved to work in a small agency, she found the right environment to support her success. Nicole found the new company culture was much more aligned with her values. "The agency is full of really bright, really smart people—really ambitious people, many who have side projects. But at the core of it, it's a team—as if it was a sports team, there's someone playing catcher, someone playing pitcher, first base, and so on. Everyone has a different role, but none of it would work well without each person doing a great job at their role, and getting along with each other." Because Nicole is collaborative, she fits well into a culture that is team oriented and consensus driven. This is the environment in which she will thrive because it aligns so well with who she is authentically.

Changes in leadership can affect the culture overnight. So keep the Magnifying Glass handy! There can be big differences in leadership and across the company. Always know what's important to the key stakeholders. Observe the behavior of your environment carefully for clues as to what is acceptable and rewarded.

Notice how the company operates and how decisions are made. Is it top-down command and control? In this hierarchical structure, you are given direction and a clear set of rules. As we discussed, these rules may be broken at times, but this culture is usually process driven.

Is the Culture Consensus Driven?

What to look for:

- Is open communication encouraged? At what level? Notice the communication chain and look for clues as to the number of people who are always in the loop and what their positions are.
- Are people rewarded for speaking up and voicing their opinions or sharing new ideas? You need to know the boundaries. It's often prudent to test the waters and see if your voice can be heard and if your opinion matters. Again, this can vary by department and team.
- Do people request your opinion? Do they act on it?
- Does the work space encourage interaction?
- Do managers have open-door policies?
- How are decisions reached?

Elizabeth recalls her experience joining a company and being unaware of the culture. When she first took the job, her supervisors asked her a lot of questions about her work. She didn't understand why, and she objected to all the questions, as she thought they were intrusive. This caused a great deal of friction between Elizabeth and her immediate supervisors. What she didn't see was the company culture was such that everyone's agreement was needed in order to make decisions. They posed the questions, not because they were micromanaging, but because her supervisors were seeking her opinion before they reached decisions. She just didn't understand the culture.

Is the Culture of Your Company Conservative?

What to look for:

- Is the technology up to date?
- What are the ages of the senior leadership team? How long have they been there?

- How do people dress?
- How innovative are their products and services?
- Are the policies, procedures, and employee benefits flexible?
- Is the company hierarchical? Are decisions driven from the top?
- What does the layout of the corporate office tell you? For instance, many traditional companies have a separate executive floor. Each senior executive has a private office, but they are isolated from their department.
- Where are the corporate headquarters located? If it's in another country, what does the culture of that country reveal about the corporate culture? Corporate culture can differ within the United States as well. A company with headquarters in the Midwest will likely be much more traditional than a company in California's Silicon Valley.

I have a few clients who work for companies that have corporate headquarters in Germany. Because these organizations are traditional and very conservative, they are most likely very slow to adapt and change.

Renee worked at a German company for a decade before calling it quits. She is ambitious and goal oriented and found that she was continually frustrated trying to get things done and initiate important changes in her department. She was not aligned with the slow-moving culture.

Political savvy can help you find allies in the company, but often your allies also get frustrated trying to make things happen. The danger for high-achieving women in slow-moving cultures is that their frustration often gets them labeled as troublemakers or complainers. Positioning yourself as part of the solution to problems is always a good career move.

If you are a high-achieving woman who finds herself in this type of environment, you will have to accept this and adapt your behavior to fit this culture or make a change. Had you considered the company culture during the interview process, you might have been better able to assess if this was the right fit for you. Political savvy will help you navigate in this culture, but you will still encounter many obstacles to advancement. For most high-achieving women, this type of culture is not a good fit and will often delay their efforts to reach their career ambitions.

Lori, who we met in Chapter 1, had to learn what it takes to work in a conservative environment: "I would be in meetings, where I would be laying out the appropriate responses and ways to do things in the credit management space—and that wasn't really in my space at that time. I was challenging people who had been working in the company for 10 years, and I was there for less than 2. And the credit group was a mess—it was an absolute disaster. So, for the process engineer that I am, it was some 'obvious as the nose on your face' kind of stuff."

"But, for whatever reason, the CFO continued to enable and support less-competent senior managers in his group. I needed to realize I should have some patience with the process and be a little bit more politically savvy, and not draw maps in crayon, as far as just how incompetent they were. I needed to trust that that would eventually have come out. I just didn't have the belief that that would happen without my highlighting it, and that's where, politically, I had a lot to learn."

This is often what happens when an ambitious woman hits walls and barriers. It is especially challenging for these women to be patient when working in conservative, slow-moving cultures. Lori learned to be more patient and accept the challenges of the workplace, and she also learned to modify her aggressive approach in order to be successful.

What Type of Behavior Is Rewarded in Your Company? As a woman in the company, look to the top and identify those women who have reached leadership positions. How do they behave? How do they communicate effectively, given the culture?

Anisha's boss is politically savvy, and Anisha watches her behavior carefully. From these observations, she has learned many valuable lessons about what it takes to succeed in her company. "I'll give you an example. When we have to deal with global and U.S. teams that have two totally different opinions, I would go to the global team and say something like, 'Listen, the United States is not going to launch this. Here are the issues they have. We need to fix these issues.' My boss would say something like, 'You know, I'm not sure if this is true, but I'm hearing inklings that the United States might not be completely aligned. I'm just a little concerned. I want everyone to feel really great about launching this thing. And I'm sure they would launch it. I'm sure it wouldn't come to a situation where they're not launching it. But, you know, here's the things that I'm hearing they might be struggling with. Do you think we could find a way to do maybe, x, y, z?"

Anisha has come to realize that her boss's softer, more inclusive approach is much more effective in dealing with the global environment. Being aware of this from watching her boss has helped Anisha modify her approach. She might think that the marketing piece the global team created was awful, but instead of directly communicating that to the team, she would say, "Oh my God, you guys did such a great job. And I know you worked really hard on this. Thank you so much. Here are a couple thoughts. You could take it or leave it; totally for you to decide, but just a couple things." Anisha has learned from observing her boss that it works to massage people a little bit more.

Nathalie came to the United States from France and took a position at a U.S.-based company. She found that her directness was not acceptable in the environment in which she worked. The French are known to be a bit more straight-in-your-face than Americans.

Nathalie would say things like, "But I don't understand. This is obvious—what don't you get?" because she thought she had already made the case. "I mean, I'm not coming up empty-handed—and not saying, 'This is why we should do it. This is what's going on in the marketplace.' So, at one point, I just said, 'Okay, guys'—as I said to my CFO—'why are you against this product?' and I realized that asking 'Why are you against this product?' is not the right way to ask the question."

In asking the question that way, Nathalie immediately put everyone, including the CFO, on the defensive. She has since learned the wisdom of observing the culture to communicate more effectively. In this case, perhaps asking the question, "What would it take for you to support this product?" would have been more productive for initiating a discussion.

What Types of Behavior Are Not Viewed Favorably? Women in every industry need to be on guard and notice what behavior can sabotage their careers. Women's behavior that is not viewed favorably often falls into two basic categories: being too emotional and being too assertive or confrontational. On the one hand, if you show your emotions in the workplace as a woman, you are considered weak, without leadership potential. You are not respected, and people believe that your emotions will trump your good judgment. Yet overly assertive and decisive women face the Double Bind we discussed in Chapter 2. If they act this way—as one would expect a leader to act—their assertive behavior gets confused with aggressiveness. Their coworkers, who believe women should be more nurturing, do not like them as a result.

Timi Hallem observes that in some workplace cultures, women make a mistake when they're overly confrontational. "Which is not to say that I think you ought to just lie down and play dead. But I think there are a lot of times when you really need to educate as much as confront. And making people get their back up or feel guilt or attacked is not a successful strategy."

"Sometimes we all are just so frustrated that we let the frustration out. And I work hard not to do that—strategy." Try to figure out a way to solve the problem or to politically get people on my side, one by one, rather than directly confronting the issue instantly, because sometimes that's not going to work. I don't let it drop; don't get me wrong. But I think, sometimes, you have to basically go like [Senator and Democratic leader] Harry Reid, round up the votes one by one—and you're not going to do that if everybody says, 'Oh, she's just so emotional. You just have to ignore her.'

"The lessons I've learned are: Give yourself a moment to absorb things before you react to them. Never cry in the office, where people can see you. If you're upset, leave, cry in your car on the way home; don't cry in front of people. It gives them too much satisfaction. And, figure out where your allies are, and use them to your tage, because there will always be jerks standing in your way. And you're going need allies to maneuver around them."

Davia Temin learned similar lessons about being emotional at work. When things fell apart for Davia and she was upset, she called up one woman she knew in that organization. "She'd been in HR. And I called her up—and I was crying. She said, 'I'm coming over,' and she came over and said, 'Okay. Here's your toolkit. You think the bathroom is to go to the bathroom. No, no, no. The bathroom is to cry. If you're going to cry, don't let anybody see you. Go for a walk, go into the bathroom— and you stick it out. I'm telling you—you stick it out. There's no doubt about it; things get tough, but they'll get better. Or they'll get worse, but whatever it is—don't walk, stick it out.' And I thought it was great advice, and I took her up on it. After all that happened to me, I managed to overcome my emotions." Davia was fortunate to have another woman tell her what behavior was unacceptable. She avoided a potentially dangerous situation by taking this woman's advice.

In any company, it's pretty safe to say that being overly emotional does not work well for women. But there are some cultures that are so hostile that it's a challenge to remain calm and cool.

Is the Culture Toxic?   I introduced you to Rita in the beginning of this chapter. She tells me that the culture of the small firm where she is employed is strict, combative, and competitive. It is common during meetings for people to lash out at one another, publically put each other down, and raise their voices. Often feeling defeated in this environment due to these dynamics, along with the fact that her boss does not support her, Rita has been brought to tears in the office. This culture is a challenging one to navigate. There are land mines everywhere for Rita.

What I am coaching Rita to do is identify and build relationships with potential allies and champions. It's obvious that her immediate boss is not going to support Rita until she produces results and meets or exceeds the revenue expectations. I have witnessed this with other clients as well. Despite the good work and good relationships, at the end of the day, it's the results that will get you the respect and visibility with senior management you need to get ahead. However, as she is working on achieving those goals, she needs to build a network of supporters—people who understand her challenges and how hard she is working.

What to look for:

- Everyone out for themselves
- Backstabbing and power plays
- No respect among coworkers; put-downs, blame games
- No advancement potential; boss does not support you and nowhere to move
- Ethical issues and potential liability
- Fighting between departments
- Gender bias among senior leadership and management

What Are the Signals That There Are Politics at Play That Are Affecting You? If you have built a strong internal network, you will be able to ask the questions to help you figure out if something is going on behind the scenes. Your allies can give you valuable information, just as Evelyn Lieberman did for Betsy Myers. That's one great benefit to having colleagues you trust. Without this information network, you can be the last one to know that your job or career is in jeopardy.

A sure sign that something is going on is that you are not included in conversations about upcoming changes in the company. Another sign is that people seem to be avoiding you. Be sensitive to behavior and communication changes.

Are you no longer included in important meetings? Are people no longer consulting with you on projects?

Take the temperature on a regular basis to avoid being blindsided. Ask your boss or trusted network for feedback. Use the Magnifying Glass to focus on shifts and changes in behavior and communication relative to you and your position.

You want to position yourself to be successful, but sometimes the environment is not supportive and is, in fact, a detriment to your career. In this case, you should be proactive and make a change to another department or another company.

Virtual Culture

We will see more organizations, especially those in global markets, transition to more virtual environments over the next decade. In their book, *Future Work: Changing Organizational Structure for the New World of Work*, authors Alison Maitland and Peter Thomson describe the new agile work environment.

They believe the workplace itself will be much more varied. We may work in a mix of office some of the time, home some of the time, or at other locations: cafés, smart-work hubs, libraries, trains, and so on. They note, "A lot of people are already working in that way, but it's just going to increase. There will be more of smart-work hubs, like little satellite offices that have the technology infrastructure—where people can work, but they're not necessarily working with colleagues from their own organization. They're working with people from other organizations who may be strangers. Offices themselves will continue to exist as locations where people meet. But they will increasingly be meeting places, rather than places where concentrated work is done."[7]

Some organizations are already adopting this new culture, but we will see many more move in this direction. How will this affect your ability to get ahead and stay ahead?

Maitland and Thomson foresee that people will be managed more by results than in the present work environment. Managing by performance and results brings new challenges. You will need to build virtual relationships in order to further your career. Those employees who are better at "virtual water cooler" behavior and who make a point of dedicating time to nurturing relationships in the absence of face-to-face encounters will do well.[8]

Because the emphasis will be placed more heavily on performance, your focus obviously will need to be on producing great results, as it should be in any organization. But don't forget about building relationships! It may be more challenging to do so in a virtual environment, but seek out ways to build and nurture relationships with people who can boost your career.

Here are some suggestions:

- During conference calls or video meetings, take notes about what people are contributing. After the meeting, send an e-mail complimenting them for their ideas and/or opinions, or commenting on the subject to stimulate ongoing conversation.
- Send a follow-up note to the attendees with related articles. Always think about ways to add value.
- Set up time to speak and/or meet one-on-one, especially when you are in close proximity.
- Set up regular meetings or conference calls with your supervisor and ask for feedback. Offer to send a weekly update showcasing your progress and issues that you would like to discuss.

Don't let the fact that you are not working in the same office deter you from doing everything you can to nurture relationships and promote your accomplishments. It's still important to make sure you are on the radar screen of those who can help you advance your career.

Summary

You've learned that the Magnifying Glass is your best friend in the workplace. Without it, you are vulnerable to the politics because you are unaware of the ever-changing dynamics. The Magnifying Glass assists you in observing the reality of the workplace relative to its power, rules, and culture.

In This Chapter, We Have Learned

- The importance of observing workplace dynamics.
- How to use the Magnifying Glass to discover who has the power and influence in the organization.
- How to use the Magnifying Glass to uncover the hidden rules.
- How to use observation skills to better understand the organization's culture and how that culture impacts your potential.

4

The Pass Go and Collect $200 Card

Strategic Networking

When I lost out on a promotion, as I described in the Introduction, I was shocked. I knew I was highly qualified and deserving of the position, but I was trumped by the politics. It took a while for me to settle down and figure out how I wanted to proceed with my career. The company offered me a lateral position that required relocation, but somehow I could not muster the energy or interest to make a move. I realized I no longer had the passion and commitment to the company, and I did not trust my job security there.

So I decided to look for an opportunity elsewhere. I perused job openings online and spoke with some headhunters who had contacted me over the years, but the most powerful move I made was to contact my network.

Right away, I got a call from Cheryl, a former colleague, who knew of a job opening at ServiceMaster to run their national homecare, pharmacy, and hospice operation. It was a high-level job, but Cheryl had connections to the management team and knew of the opening because she worked in another business unit at that firm. Cheryl and I had worked together in another company, so she was aware of my expertise. She made a call on my behalf and told them about my background and experience. In fact, she pre-sold me! I then sent a résumé, started the interviewing process, and landed the job.

The point is that Cheryl, a former colleague with whom I stayed in touch over the years, opened the door for me and helped me to secure the new position. I never would have known that ServiceMaster was looking for someone to run this company had it not been for her. This is the power of a network!

We can sometimes lapse into a victim mentality and think unfortunate things happen to us in the workplace. We get fired. We lose out on a promotion. The company goes bankrupt or moves operations out of our area. But the fact of the matter is we can take control of our career destiny in many ways. It does, however, take strategy, focus, and intention. One of the most powerful ways to build a successful career and take control of your destiny is to proactively build a strategic network. That's where the Pass Go Card comes in. The Pass Go Card in your Political Toolkit is strategic networking.

For those of you who are familiar with Monopoly, you know winning the game takes a lot of strategy and planning. And when you are fortunate enough to pull the Pass Go and Collect $200 Card, it helps position you to win. Not only do you advance around the board faster, but also you are rewarded with a bonus of $200! It's a great feeling when you pick the Pass Go Card due to the advantage it provides. Your strategic network functions the same way. It positions you to win. The only difference between winning at Monopoly and building a strong network and successful career is that the focus of your strategy is to get ahead, but not at the expense of others, as in Monopoly. That's poor politics.

The Pass Go Card is an important tool in your political toolkit, because building a strategic network and nurturing relationships help you to get ahead and stay ahead. It's not enough to reach your career goal. Your network of strong relationships will help protect you to maintain your status over time.

Networking proactively is important. What happens if you don't have a strong network and suddenly you lose your job? If you don't have a network to tap into, you're out of luck. It will most likely take you much longer to find a new position. If you're involved in a power play at work and need to build support for your position, and you don't have a support network, it's too late. If you are trying to build consensus for a new idea or initiative and you don't have allies behind you, it's difficult to do. And how can you get information about a hiring manager or new boss if you don't have a network of people to provide that information? The Pass Go Card provides the advantage by supporting you with a powerful collection of people who are willing and able to speak for you.

Here's how the Pass Go Card helps you advance faster toward your goal.

1. There is a direct relationship between networking strategically and increased income.

    Upwardly Mobile, Inc., with the support of Pepperdine University's Graziadio School of Business Management, conducted research in April 2008 about how professionals use networking. They surveyed more than 600 high-earning "elite" professionals about how they use networking to cultivate richer relationships, gain more access, and enjoy more success in their careers and personal lives. Their findings confirmed that "networking is a key driver behind higher salaries and career advancement."[1]

    For me, there is no better validation of this fact than my own experience, when networking helped me find a position running a national company. My compensation almost doubled! Tapping into your network usually pays off. If you have a strong network, it will give you the opportunity to supercharge your salary and career.

2. Your strategic network helps to promote you and refer you for new opportunities. Often your champions do a better job promoting you than you can do for yourself!

    Carolyn Lawrence, CEO of Women of Influence, commented about this: "I'm always asking other female CEOs, how do they build relationships? How do they get big, new clients or referrals and promotions? And it's often because they've had a champion who can talk about them better than they can talk about themselves. Women are so modest; we tend to not really share and talk about how great we are, how talented we are. So sometimes, this is the champion's role, our cheerleader, and for women especially, this is something you really need in your back pocket."

I have heard many stories from some of my well-connected clients how they have used their network to help them find new positions. Lisa's story stands out because her network helped her find another high-level position within 60 days!

Lisa had invested many years in the banking industry and had reached a senior position, but she decided to take a risk and leave banking to become the COO of a technology startup. It seemed like a great opportunity to leverage her skills and move into an equity position. After a short time, it became apparent that this new opportunity was not working out very well. Her CEO was not supportive and became increasingly difficult and distant. Her gut told her she was on her way out, and her gut was right. After just one year, the CEO asked her to step down.

Lisa is the primary breadwinner in her family. She commanded a high salary and had been compensated very well, but now she had the challenge of finding another senior executive position, and she was frightened.

The one thing Lisa had going for her, besides her incredible track record and talent, was a powerful and supportive network. Once she notified her contacts that she was looking for a position back in banking, amazing things started to happen. Her network responded with leads for openings in several institutions and, in fact, some of the jobs had not even been posted yet—another great advantage of using her Pass Go Card. She secured another top position in a month and a half! That's the power of a strategic network.

I have looked to my network for business opportunities as well. When I was consulting with a startup technology company in 2001, I was tasked with finding a beta partner for their new platform. It's not easy to sell this type of partnership. It takes a huge commitment of time and resources for the company involved in the beta. They need to have a great deal of trust to enter into this arrangement. The first place I looked was my network. I called some of my previous colleagues whom I had stayed in touch with who knew me well, and I was able to quickly find a company willing to engage in this partnership. My network did not let me down!

3. Network contacts give you critical information about the workplace, the people, and the politics. This information is not always readily available and is only passed along to trusted colleagues. Building a network that provides you with this information is important for developing your political savvy.

You can tap into your network to get information about key people in the workplace. For instance, maybe you are posting for a new position and you want to know more about the hiring manager or the decision makers and influencers. Trusted colleagues can provide such information to help position you. They may even endorse you for the promotion.

If you are trying to build consensus for a new initiative or work your way through a political situation, your network can help you determine your allies or potential obstacles. Information networks are powerful for these purposes.

Megan found out about her new job as head of business development at an investment firm through strategic networking. She mentioned to one of her contacts that she wanted to move back home to Boston. She not only got information about a job opening, but she also got important information about the company before she interviewed. "I had really good insight on the firm before I even came into the interview. I knew about the personalities. I knew about the people. I knew about the culture.

I had to meet everyone. I interviewed all the partners. I met other people on the team. I did reference calls on them. They did reference calls on me. It was still a risk, but it was a better-informed risk than it was when I took a job prior to this. And I felt comfortable taking the risk I was taking."

Your strategic network positions you for success!

Women and Networking

Women are natural networkers, but they do not necessarily network to support their professional growth, which puts them at a tremendous disadvantage to men who know how to work the system. The reality is that we don't approach networking with much thought or planning.

Here are three ways you can step up your networking skills:

Be Strategic

Thinking strategically to build a network that supports your career goal is one of the most powerful things you can do to get ahead and stay ahead. Too often, networking efforts are just social, haphazard, and as a result, ineffective. You make friends and connections, but these people are not always in a position to help you further your career or—most important—they may not be willing to speak for you.

One of the pitfalls many women encounter in business is their failure to network strategically. Barbara Annis & Associates referred to this in their white paper, *Solutions to Women's Advancement*: "While men network for transactional reasons, women will network for relational reasons. That is, men will network to obtain something, while women network for relationships and connections."[2]

They quoted one executive woman in their report. "At an investment bank's triennial event, a woman senior leader looked forward to reconnecting with colleagues from around the world; she was therefore stunned to see them looking past her or over her head during their conversations."

"They all had their eyes on the door, waiting for the new CEO to enter so they could race over to introduce themselves. She felt deflated that her colleagues were more interested in positioning themselves than wanting to reconnect and left the reception. Only later did she realize her own foolishness in not seizing the strategic opportunity her colleagues did."[3]

As an example, Julie, who we met in Chapter 3, realized her male colleague got his promotion because he was doing a great deal of networking and was strategic about his approach, which proved to be very effective. "When I came back from my maternity leave, he told me, 'Oh yeah, I interviewed with him and her, and I've been talking and grabbing coffee with such-and-such.' And I realized, 'Oh, wow. Okay, he's really networking within the firm. And as a result, he got the promotion, with a good team. I didn't get the promotion.'"

This realization of how strategic her male colleague was about his networking activity was an eye opener for Julie. She saw the results of his efforts pay off, and she quickly changed her own mind-set about building relationships in the workplace.

Don't Limit Your Networking to People You Know and Like

To network effectively, you need to move out of your comfort zone and identify people who can help your career, not just those people you like. Strategic networking is more than socializing and swapping business cards; it's creating solid relationships inside and outside the company to support your career aspirations. It takes focus and intention to build such a network, but it's invaluable for your professional development.

Research validates that men and women approach networking differently. The fact that women limit their networking to people they like and know is cited as one reason women don't advance at the same rate as men. It also influences their compensation and bonuses. "Indeed, it might not be who or what you know that creates advantage, but rather more simply, who you become by dint of how you hang out—the disadvantaged hang out with folks just like themselves, while the advantaged engage folks of diverse opinion and practice."[4]

Highly open networks tie together a diverse set of individuals who don't know one another. This type of network is often associated with faster promotions, higher bonuses, and strong performance reviews. Men are more likely to have these open, efficient networks and at least twice as likely as women to say that they look for relationships at work that can help them get on the right assignments and get ahead.

Highly closed networks are made up of people you know who also know each other. Women and people of color are more likely to have these networks, which are not effective in supporting their advancement.

Look at your current network. Is it open or closed (see Figure 4.1)?

Do you tend to network only with people you know and like? You are missing out on the opportunity to move your career forward faster! This is another reason why the Pass Go Card is important. It gives you a strategic focus. If you use your card wisely, you will see dramatic results. Keep it in your pocket at all times so you can draw on it when you need it.

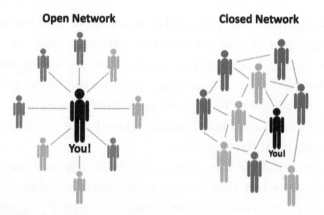

FIGURE 4.1 Open vs. Closed Network

Leverage Your Relationships

Have you ever accumulated thousands of airline miles and then had them expire before you could cash them in? This is a great metaphor for women and networking. We build relationships, and we are eager to please and help others, so we accumulate "favors" like airline miles, but we never cash them in. We never ask for anything in return, and as a result, we lose the power of quid pro quo.

The Center for Work-Life Policy comments on this: "To their detriment, women perceive cultivating relationships and mobilizing them on their behalf as, at best, an occasional necessity rather than the *very exercise of leadership*. They fail to see that the practice of seeking out powerful people, cultivating their favor, and cashing in those chips *is itself a demonstration of leadership potential*" [italics in original].[5]

Carolyn Lawrence, CEO of Women of Influence, talks about paying it forward and leveraging relationships: "If there's someone that you'd like advice from, is there anything you can do for them? Or, is there something in your conversation where you can suggest things that might be helpful? Can you help connect them with someone? Can you help get them a job? Can you help them meet someone that's in your circle that they wouldn't have access to? This can often be very helpful, because women like to give, and add value, and be doers, and be helpful, so it's certainly a strength that I like to lean on when I'm connecting or networking: 'What can I do for you?' Because once you see how good I am and how much you can trust me, you're going to want to help me too when the time is right."

Lisa is a master at paying it forward. We learned earlier how, when she lost her job, she was able to tap into her network and get some leads for new opportunities. But Lisa always invested time and energy in her network. "I came late to the game of understanding what networking was about. And I've tried to, now, tell everybody, every young person that I meet that your network is everything. There was a belief in my mind, given the fact that I wasn't good at networking, that calling someone after five or six years just to say, 'I need a job,' was being rude, because I hadn't talked to that person. And that was just really silly. And the way I get around that—and the way I, in my head, know that that's not silly—is that, when someone calls me after six or seven years, I help them, if I can. Or I try to, or I try to be nice about it and just make sure that I give them some time—so that I know that I've given them the consideration that they need. When you do that, you realize that when you give, you can take. So, it all just comes around in a circle."

"What I've done through the years is, most of the people I network with and have in my network genuinely like me, and I genuinely like them. And it's because I've done good work for them, or I've helped them, or when they've asked me for help for somebody else, I've tried. So, it's good business sense to actually be a good business partner to all these people."

Women are naturally giving, but you don't want to be a doormat. You are leaving opportunities on the table by not asking for help when you need it.

Linda Descano, an executive at Citi who we met in Chapter 1, says she doesn't just ask people to do something for her because she's done something for them. She is very savvy about who she asks and how she asks. "I don't say, 'Oh, but I did this for you.' But I will go to people and say, 'You know, I'm struggling with an issue,' or 'I'm trying to better understand x. Can you help me? Who would be the person that you would recommend? Or can you connect me to someone?' Yes, I have cashed in my political capital. And sometimes, I go to people that I've built relationships with through my random acts of kindness. And in other cases, it's a bit of a cold call. And I've found people are very helpful when you're gracious in your asking and you are specific in terms of why you're asking them, and mindful of their time."

Linda also takes the time to send a special handwritten thank-you note when people do go out of their way and provide her the assistance she requested. She doesn't take their helpfulness for granted. This is a great way to continue to build and nurture trusting relationships with your network.

I have heard from many well-connected women that they continually invest in their network, and when they pay it forward, it pays off. It paid off for Lisa, Megan, and me when we tapped our networks for leads on jobs and new business opportunities. Both Megan and Lisa told me that they always take calls from their colleagues or respond to their e-mails. They always make time because they appreciate the value of their contacts. This time is generously given but pays off in spades. Paying it forward pays off. When you are willing to make the time for your colleagues, they will return the favor in kind. And if you make a request, and someone does not respond positively, that's okay, too. Don't take it personally. Just move on; that's why having an expansive network is beneficial.

The Upwardly Mobile/Pepperdine study cited earlier found that "elite professionals know what most 'networking' professionals do not: that effective networking today is about quickly cutting through the clutter and creating meaningful online and offline connections, relationships, and rapport—the kind that enable the giving and receiving of trust."[6]

The study also found that "truly effective networking—networking in the manner of the high-earning and high-career-level elite professionals represented within this study—requires more than 'connections' or 'friends'; it requires cutting through clutter and focusing on what matters—real, mutually beneficial partnerships."[7]

The Pass Go Card helps you to establish these mutually beneficial partnerships to support your career efforts. Identifying the right people—those people who have power and influence and who are willing to recommend you—is the first step. Building and nurturing relationships of trust is the next step. The third important step is to fill your "favor bank" by finding ways to help others and then leverage these relationships by asking for assistance when you need it.

Finding the Right People: Who Do You Know, and Who Do You Need to Know?

Look strategically at your workplace to identify contacts who will help you build visibility and credibility to support your career and promote you for new opportunities as they arise.

In Chapter 3, we discussed using the Magnifying Glass to take a close look at the workplace and the ever-changing dynamics. We made a note of those who have the power and influence to help you, whether it is for a promotion, a high-potential or sponsorship program, or special projects to give you visibility. We also observed the people who are supportive of women advancing and potential allies. Now is the time to pull out your notes from Chapter 3 and review your list of influential people as we begin to develop a concrete networking plan.

Looking at your entire organization may seem a bit daunting, so let's narrow the focus by dividing the workplace into three basic categories of contacts: operational, developmental, and strategic, shown in Figure 4.2.

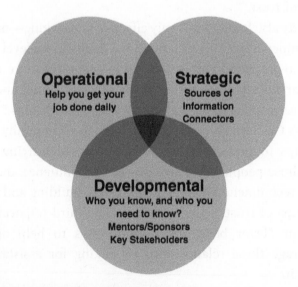

FIGURE 4.2 Workplace Networks

As you can see, the three categories of contacts overlap. You may have people who fit into more than one category or who change categories over time. In other words, how they function as part of your strategy may change.

Let's take a better look at these categories.

1. Operational

    The people who fall into this category are the people you work with every day. They help you get your job done. They may be on your team, in your department, or in support roles in the company. Such support roles might be sales, marketing, IT, or HR. In other words, you don't necessarily work directly with them all the time, but your jobs overlap at times. You need them to do your job.

    Look at your workplace and write a list of all the people you interact with on a regular basis to determine if there are some important connections for you here.

2. Developmental (Decision Makers, Influencers)

    These contacts can serve as role models, potential mentors, or sponsors. They have power and influence over decisions that affect your career. They are decision makers and are often key stakeholders in that business.

    You may not have a strong enough relationship with some of these contacts to know for sure if they are willing to be your sponsor or mentor, but identifying them and placing them in your network plan is important. You will then develop a strategic plan to build relationships with these people over time.

3. Strategic (Connectors)

    Your strategic contacts serve as sources of information and connection. They can also provide operational and developmental support. These people open up doors for you and provide introductions to other people in all categories.

Let's say you have a project stalled in IT and you are speaking with one of your colleagues about your frustration. She offers to connect you with a guy in the IT department whom she knows well who can help you move your project forward. She makes the call on your behalf, and presto, your project magically gets his attention and is completed quickly. That's what a connector can do for you.

Strategic contacts also can feed you important information about the workplace politics and help you avoid potential land mines. They can introduce you to the key stakeholders on your list that you don't know well enough to approach on your own. Strategic contacts are vital to the success of your network.

Having these three categories helps you to see the bigger picture and to find people across the organization with whom you interact or who should be included in your strategic network.

When Mia had difficulty with the HR executive in her company and did not have support from the CEO, as we mentioned in Chapter 3, she tried to build allies across the organization to support her efforts. She realized quickly her allies either didn't have the power, the ability, or, ultimately, the will to help her. So it is important to identify the right people for your network. The contacts in your power network should have a purpose as a decision maker, influencer, or connector/source of information.

Upwardly Mobile states, "It is our view—and the view of the highest-earning professionals in our study—that the single most critical factor in determining the value of your network is breadth of connections *with the right people*—people willing to recommend. If individuals within your network are not willing to recommend you, they are of no, and possibly even negative, value to your network. If individuals within your network—some of whom you may have developed deep relationships with—are not willing to recommend you and may even speak negatively about you, they in fact detract from the value of your network."[8]

Building a Power Network That Supports Your Career Goal

The place to begin any strategic plan is with a goal or intention. So we start this network plan in the same manner. It starts with your career goal, short or long term. This is a necessary first step. How can you put a support system in place for an unidentified purpose?

You don't need to worry about identifying an exact title or position. It may, in fact, be somewhat vague in terms of title, but you should have an idea of where you want to go in your organization. The more specific you can be about your goal, the easier it will be to identify a power network to support it.

What role are you seeking? What kind of responsibility does it have? You can refer back to the Bridging the Gap worksheet in Chapter 3 (Figure 3.2) to see all the requirements to assume this new role.

Things to consider after identifying your goal:

- Who does this position report to?
- Does it require a move to another business unit?
- What are the politics involved in making the move?
- Who are the decision makers involved in making this happen?
- Who are the people who would influence this decision?
- What is the reality of how your organization promotes people?
- If you need additional experience or resources, who are the people who can help you get this?
- Who are the people who will support you in this goal?
- Who are the people who will not support you in this goal?
- If there are people who will not support you, what relationships can you develop that will circumvent them?

Your Power Network

Your Power Network will consist of individuals who can help you achieve your career goal. By now you should have several lists of people in your workplace: those with power and influence, the decision makers and influencers, and the people who are able to connect you with others (they know everything about everybody) or provide you with information.

You also have a good understanding of the unwritten rules and how promotions actually happen in your organization. This knowledge helps you build a network of the right people to support your goal.

Last, you have identified a goal, and along with that goal, you have noted the people you need to build relationships with to make this happen.

Now let's put this all together and build your Power Network (see Figure 4.3)!

First, list all your contacts and potential contacts in the left column. Review all the information you have about them, and in the "Function" column, identify those people who are decision makers for your career advancement or key stakeholders, and mark them "A."

Next, identify all those people who are influencers. These people have great relationships with decision makers. They have the ear of senior management. Again, please remember this is specifically designed to support your career goal. Mark them "B" in the "Function" column.

Name	Function (A, B, C)	Influence (1-10)	Relationship (1-10)
1.			
2.			
3.			
4.			
5.			
6.			
7.			
8.			
9.			
10.			
11.			
12.			

FIGURE 4.3 Your Power Network

Last, identify those people who are in the strategic category, the connectors. They have information; they have great connections and can introduce you to some of the influencers and decision makers you have identified. Mark them "C."

Remember, these people may function in more than one role. So you may have influencers who are also connectors. In that case, list all their functions, "B" and "C."

Go through the entire list of your contacts, and under the "Influence" column, rank them based on how powerful and influential they are in helping you reach your desired goal. The scale is from 1 to 10, with 10 meaning they have direct power over the decision and 1 indicating they have no influence that you know of. (I would find it difficult to justify why someone with a ranking of 1 is even on your list unless you feel you need to gather more information to validate their influence.)

Now, look at each entry and rate the strength of your connection with them in the third column, "Relationship." The scale is from 1 to 10, with 10 indicating a very strong relationship because they know you and your value proposition. A ranking of 1 means you have no connection with them at this time. They don't know you and probably don't know "of" you.

The next step is to compare the two ranking categories and analyze your results. Obviously, someone who has a high ranking in power and influence would be your priority, but how well do you know them? How well do they know you? You need to create a plan to begin building and nurturing these relationships. Please stretch your comfort zone and identify at least one decision maker or influencer whom you don't know and who requires an introduction.

If you don't know some of the decision makers or key stakeholders on the list, look at your strategic contacts or connectors. Who can introduce you or give you critical information about the decision makers? These people should be a top priority to connect with as well. Continue to add to your list of connectors, for these are the people who will help you forge relationships where you have none.

What you have just completed is your strategic plan. Treat it like a sales plan for your career advancement. Prioritize contacts based on their power and influence or as sources of information, and make it your intention to meet or strengthen relationships with these people. Figure out the best way to reach out to them through your connectors. Ask questions about the most appropriate way to communicate with them and how often.

And last, keep a record of all your activity, including dates of conversations and e-mails so that you can follow up and stay on track. Many of my well-connected clients keep spreadsheets with this information.

Davia Temin has always used her network to her advantage in business. She keeps track of all the conversations she's had with important people she meets. "I get a lot of business that way; that's the only way I get business—through my network and through all the people who I know. So, the one thing I can tell you that I think is good advice is: I keep the name of everybody with whom I've had a substantive conversation—or who I meet who is impressive to me, or maybe I impressed. I have a humongous database, and I keep in touch with people. I've done that since Columbia—so I've done that my entire career. And I have all those names. I used to keep them in Rolodexes. And, when I was in one job, I must've had 30 of those Rolodexes of 500 or 1,000 in them. There was not enough room in the office. When I got to GE (General Electric), at one point at a very senior level, one of the guys came in and said, 'What are all these things?' And I said, 'Well, these are all the people I know.' He said, 'Well, can't you get them on the computer?'" She finally was able to do so.

The point is that Davia created a way to keep track of the people she meets and is able to easily access their contact information. Find a solution that meets your needs: a spreadsheet, Rolodex, or perhaps a customer relationship management application such as GoldMine or Salesforce.com.

Your Networking Mind-Set

As much as women are likely to be social and enjoy meeting other like-minded people, I also recognize that something holds them back from building connections at business-related networking events. Could it be their mind-set about networking?

Women of Influence in Canada ran a focus group a couple of years ago with emerging women leaders for the purpose of figuring out ways to help women make connections at networking events.

Carolyn Lawrence, the CEO, commented. "It's mind-boggling because these women are so amazing, but then they get to a networking event, and they just stand cemented to the floor with the girls they came in with."

In the focus group, they asked these women if they liked networking, and overwhelmingly the response was "No." Lawrence says, "We then asked, 'Do you understand the importance of networking to build your career potential?' Their answer was, of course, 'Yes.' So then we asked, 'Okay. Do you enjoy connecting with other women to advance your career potential?' Their response was 'Yes.' So, is it a shift in perception? I think that's part of it. And, for whatever reason, *networking* as a word has a bad reputation. We don't like it; we find it kind of dirty, and we cringe. And we don't want to feel like we're doing shallow business development."

Networking is simply meeting and building relationships with people. It's really no different than getting to know someone in any other situation. Changing your mind-set about networking opens the door to many powerful opportunities to meet and connect with people who can help you reach your career goal.

Find Commonality

One of the most frequent questions I am asked about networking is how I initially approach people. What do I say? How do I build connections? We can get paralyzed when we think we need an "elevator pitch" to introduce ourselves—that we need to memorize some special introduction to make a great first impression. For some reason, we believe that networking for business is different from what we know about getting to know people in general. It's not.

The fact of the matter is that when you show an interest in another person, you are making a great first impression. It is not and should not be about you. That's the quickest way to turn someone off. Finding some commonality creates an instant connection.

Carolyn Lawrence advises women to "find the commonality and start talking about it. And don't leave that person until you've made the connection. But once you have, get going, exchange cards. Make plans to talk about it another time. And then go find another connection. It's a whole body experience. It's so much more fulfilling for both of you, and you get so much further ahead because of it."

Lisa told me about a woman in her company who was politically savvy in building relationships with the men in her company. They all played golf, and she didn't like golf, but she was an avid sports fan, and she found this was something they had in common. She would have conversations with them during the week about all the sporting events that happened over the weekend, and it gave her an "in." She found the commonality with which to build relationships.

Because Anisha works in a very large company, she can identify people who might be influential, but her challenge is approaching them and building a connection. "If I have nothing to do with their division, their role, or I don't at all work with them or interface with them, how do I create a relationship in a way that doesn't feel like manipulation and using, but feels more organic and natural?"

Think about when you first meet someone new. Aren't you more engaged in the conversation when that person is interested in learning more about you? It's human nature. You apply this same principle when you meet new people in business. Ask questions to learn more about them. Listen for some commonality, and the conversation will flow from there.

Find Out What They Want and Need

We first met Katie in Chapter 1. Katie hired me to help her secure a new position in another division of her company. In Chapter 2, I described the process by which Katie identified her value proposition. Next I coached her to look at the organization and identify people who had power and influence in the business units that interested her. This was the first stage of her strategic network plan.

Once she identified those people, she worked with her influencers and connectors to get information about them and their department. She asked her network for introductions to the people she wanted to meet. But if that didn't work, she made appointments to meet them regardless. She would simply identify herself and what department she worked in, and ask for a short meeting to better understand what they did in their division.

When she met with them, she asked questions. She showed her interest in learning more about them and their work. Her initial approach with them was that she was unaware of what they did in their department and wanted to know more. What were they working on? What were their goals? What were some of their current projects? Did they have any projects that were a challenge? What were the challenges?

Once she got all this information, she could easily figure out how she might help them based on her value proposition, which was her technical expertise and business experience. Once she understood the business goals and objectives, she offered to assist them in finding a technology solution to solve their problem. This is effective on several levels. First, her interest in them and their work helps create an initial bond. Her offer to help pays it forward. When she volunteers to help them, they learn firsthand about her value. At the same time, she is building credibility and visibility with key stakeholders across the

FIGURE 4.4 How You Add Value

company. It's a win-win situation that starts with understanding your value, as you can see in Figure 4.4.

Filling Your Favor Bank

The example of Katie networking across the organization demonstrates how you can go from your value proposition (the Mirror) to identifying key stakeholders (the Magnifying Glass) to building a strategic network of relationships (the Pass Go Card). All the tools in the Political Toolkit work together to promote you in an effective, savvy manner.

What do your stakeholders need? Offering to help and do favors is an effective way to build relationships of trust and influence with your key stakeholders.

Elizabeth says this has worked well for her. "I've always tried to get into an organization and then find out what are others' pet peeve or project that they can never seem to get around to doing. And if I can help take that roadblock off their pathway, I find a way to help them solve their problem. Sometimes it's not even been in my area of expertise. I've done it where I've had to go learn something to then go solve that problem. But I knew they were an influence maker."

Chris Reilly, a senior executive in the financial industry, also talks about how she ingratiated herself to the key stakeholders in the organization by taking on projects no one else would do. "I took on certain jobs or tasks because I knew, or I had a sense that, the guy at the top of the house really cared. And some of the guys didn't want to touch it with a 10-foot pole, because it was hairy or it was a business line that was bleeding losses, or had problems, or it was too small. And I kind of felt that (A) it gives me a broader experience, and (B) it puts me on some higher-level person's radar screen. Therefore, it's probably worth doing and doing well. And if it matters to the CEO or the COO and I can help them, maybe they'll see what stuff I'm made of."

Where are the opportunities in your organization to help and do favors for the people who have power and influence? Look for these opportunities with your Magnifying Glass. It's a great way to build relationships of trust, as others will see the value you bring to the organization. Ingratiating yourself to others is another way to collect favors in your favor bank that you can cash in when you need them.

How and When to Network

The first question I get asked during my workshops on strategic networking is about time management. How do I find the time to network? I can't network after work. I can't spend the time during the evenings to network for business; that's my time with my family.

I've also heard from my clients, especially those in traditional financial institutions, that men are often uncomfortable going out to dinner with them. The men are very sensitive about socializing with a woman who works for them and are very careful about their reputation. If you are in a similar situation, find a way to spend one-on-one time with the important people in your network. Be creative.

Everyone will find his or her own solution to the challenges about how and when to network. I often suggest that once you identify the person you want to get to know better, schedule a lunch or coffee during the day and have a one-on-one conversation. There should be no excuse that you don't have time to build these important relationships. Make it your intention to do it. Be strategic about your time and targets. Some women do business lunches, dinners, or coffee dates. Some learn to play golf. The point is that you must figure out what works best for you, but don't use the excuse that you cannot network because of time constraints. Remember, the Pass Go Card is a powerful way to advance and earn more money.

Davia Temin did her networking during the workday. She took great advantage of the officer's dining room to have lunch meetings. When she first took the position running marketing for the North American Corporate Finance Division of a bank, she discovered that she could bring people to lunch there every day for free. Her mentor thought this was a great opportunity. As Davia tells it, he said, "'This is very impressive.' And I said, 'Yeah, it is, isn't it?' He said, 'Can you bring anybody you want here?' And I said, 'Yeah.' And he said, 'As much as you want?' And I said, 'Yeah.' He said, 'Okay. Well, you're going to bring somebody different here every single day, five days a week, four weeks a month, 12 months a year. This is so impressive that you can do this and that you're at this level. And that's what you're going to do.' And I looked at him and said, 'Yeah, but Bob, someday I want to have a slice of pizza and get my shoes fixed, you know?' And he went, 'All right, four days a week.'"

Networking outside the office can be more of a challenge for women, so it is very important to be strategic about your time. I take the time to find groups and organizations that will offer me the most value. I will try to go to one or two meetings before I make a commitment to join. In this way, I can determine if the organization is a good fit.

Carolyn Lawrence has a young child and tries to balance being home at night with her family and her need to network as an entrepreneur. She says she picks one or two clubs that she wants to be a member of each year where she knows her key people will be. "And I pick my moments. I might pick not more than two events per week to be out outside business hours. But the next step is critical, too. So you pick where you're going and then you prepare. Who's going to be in the room? What is my intention for this event? Who do I want to speak to? What do I want to tell them? What does success look like at this event? If I can go in there and accomplish my intention in five minutes, I'm out of there."

Many women choose to strengthen their relationships with colleagues outside the office. Though this may be a challenge because of the time constraints, it is extremely beneficial to strengthen the relationships that are important to you.

Chris Reilly discovered that most senior executive men played golf in her industry, and it was the optimal way for her to build important business relationships. "I always did a lot of internal networking because I always wanted to know what's going on. And so, I would always ask peers or subordinates to lunch, or occasionally, even superiors, to establish a relationship. I absolutely did not do enough external networking until too late in my career. I chalked it up to time management, but in retrospect, it's something women need to do sooner rather than later if they want to get ahead. And I just didn't do it. I worked long hours, came home to my three kids, and did my second shift, which was probably pretty typical. If I had to do it all over again, I would definitely learn to play golf sooner. Because when you spend four hours in a golf cart with somebody, (A) you really get to know them, and (B) there's an awful lot of informal information that gets shared, especially after a couple of beers. You learn a lot about them as individuals, too."

"In some of the organizations golf may not be a big part of the culture, but it is in investment banking; that's when I really started playing a lot of golf. I was the head of corporate development and all these guys asked me to play golf with them. I was literally working on the golf course."

Marilyn Tam also found that golf offers an opportunity to talk about business in ways that won't happen sitting in a meeting at work. She says she finds out a lot about people on the golf course. "Do they cheat in golf? You'll find an amazing number of people do! And it's not a big cheat—it's like, when a ball drops, do they just kick it, you know, a little bit to get it out of the really rough? Or do they put one less stroke on that hole? I mean, small things and big things: Do they gamble on the holes? How competitive are they?

"And it helps so much in the work, because you understand now what makes them get motivated, what makes them nervous, what makes them excited, what makes them frustrated. So, you can understand how to work with them in a way that wouldn't be obvious otherwise. And, ultimately, that's going to help both your work and the other person's work, as well as the company. So, it's really very beneficial."

The informal conversations that take place with colleagues outside the office often reveal more about its dynamics and politics. As your relationships get stronger, you will learn invaluable information about the workplace that will help you position yourself. You may also learn about new opportunities, especially if you have connections with people who have power and influence.

Your External Network

Another powerful network to support your career advancement exists outside the workplace. Once you begin to think more strategically about building connections, some of these opportunities will become more obvious. Consider expanding your network to include:

1. Alumni from college or graduate school

    Stay connected to former alumni. Follow them on social media. If they live locally, set up time to meet with them. Where do they work? What are they doing? They just might be a source of information about a new company in the future. You might be able to help them as well.

    If you have a local alumni association, go to meetings and meet new people or reconnect with others. Often these get-togethers are great for networking purposes.

2. Community-based organizations

    We discussed in Chapter 2 how volunteer work in your community can help you gain visibility. These organizations also provide great access to business owners, entrepreneurs, and people with similar interests. You can build some influential relationships through your involvement.

3. Nonprofit boards

This is a wonderful way to give back and meet new people. Often board members are well-connected people with influence. Once they get to know you and what you can offer, they function as connectors and influencers.

4. Industry-related groups

As business networking has become more commonplace, the number of professional organizations has dramatically increased. Some are women only, and some may be specific to your industry. Do some research and also ask around to see which groups make the most sense for you and your career goal. As I mentioned earlier, go to a couple of meetings before joining an organization and see if the organization is a good fit for you.

These networking groups also offer great volunteer opportunities that are a terrific way to meet people. Whether it's working on event planning, a program committee, or membership, there are many ways you can offer to help and get to know people better. These people might be of assistance to you or vice versa in the future.

Make sure you collect people's business cards and write a note on the back about your conversation. If you simply give your own business card away, you are also giving away the control of the follow-up activity. Make sure you follow up promptly so that they remember your conversation, especially if you offered to do something for them.

Online Networking

One would think that because we are constantly connected online, networking online is easy. After all, we have the potential for tremendous exposure to a tremendous network of people. However, online professional networking is not without challenges.

First, it is difficult to cut through all the noise. The number of people who connect with us is daunting, and as a result, it's easy to lose our strategic focus. Someone approaches us on Facebook, Twitter, LinkedIn, or any other social network and asks to connect, and our first response is to say "Okay." We end up with a huge network of people we don't know and who offer us no value. It's wiser to look carefully at their profiles to determine if you want that person in your network. If you determine there is some commonality, then reply and set up some time to talk and initiate a relationship. The point is that the number of contacts in your online network is not nearly as important as the quality. Ask yourself if you can establish a mutually beneficial relationship with that person.

The next challenge is managing your online presence. Does your profile reflect your value proposition? Think more about how you can communicate what you have contributed to organizations in which you have worked rather than posting a résumé that lists all the positions you've held. Think carefully about your heading on LinkedIn and your description on Twitter. How can you add value to your online network?

I am always thinking about how I can add value to my online network and, in doing so, demonstrate my expertise. Connecting with like-minded people is a great first step. Then learn what might interest them. On LinkedIn, I join groups that have my target audience for coaching, speaking, and writing. These groups, mostly of professional women, appreciate when I share articles, my blog, and podcasts, or pose questions to stimulate conversation. I try to comment on other people's postings as well. People begin to recognize you for your contribution, and it's a good way to connect further with individuals.

On Twitter, I find it especially challenging to keep my strategic focus. There is a lot of noise and clutter on Twitter! You can manage your connections by putting them into different groups. I have one group labeled "professional women"; another might be "media" or "friends." Think strategically about how you respond to others and how you can start ongoing conversations.

One of the biggest challenges in social media is managing your reputation. Because of this, executive coach and author, Dr. Lois Frankel, calls social media a double-edged sword. "On the one hand, it can help you in many ways. On the other hand, once it's out there, you can't put the toothpaste back in the tube. You have to assume that everything you put in social media is eventually going to come up over the course of your lifetime."

Lois gave me a powerful example of how social media can catch up with you. She told me the story about a young woman who had worked for her and had asked her for a reference. She was interviewing for a job at a very prestigious university. She was about to be offered the job, and the vice president of this particular office called Lois and said, "I got your reference and I appreciate it. I just have one question for you. Do you think she might do anything that could embarrass our institution?" Lois was surprised by the question because this woman never did anything to embarrass her or her firm, and so she asked what he meant. It turned out that part of their interview process was to do an extensive Google search, and they discovered some pictures of her when she was in college.

Lois said, "I don't know if it was a wet T-shirt contest, but she was drinking beer, and she had body piercings, and he came up with the photo." Lois explained to him that the photo was 10 years old and that she had matured in the past seven years while working for Lois. But the point is that once photos are out there, they are there forever, and you need to manage your reputation. You also need to realize that many companies now do Google searches on their candidates and look for clues that the person may not have the best judgment or may not be the best fit culturally.

Social media is a powerful way to build a positive online presence and connections. This not only promotes you but also helps you expand your network and visibility. If you stay focused and strategic, you will master how to overcome the challenges associated with sifting through the online clutter. Your focus should be making mutually beneficial connections based on your positive online presence.

Building Relationships across Cultures

As companies become more agile in the future, there will be an increased opportunity for you to work virtually. The less face time you have with colleagues, the more challenging it is to build and maintain a network of relationships. I offered some suggestions for building virtual relationships in Chapter 3.

What adds to the complexity of building virtual relationships is when there are cultural differences. It is not uncommon for many companies today to have global teams that represent a variety of countries. In this environment, you need to first understand the cultural differences before you can begin to establish relationships of trust. For instance, In China, Japan, and Korea, drinking alcohol—and a lot of it—is important to building trust. The sentiment is, "Because we drink a lot of alcohol, you really show me deeply who you are, and that you have nothing to hide."[9]

By contrast, the way to build relationships in Brazil, Russia, and India is to create an emotional connection. If you don't invest significant time in developing close relationships, you won't be able to develop the trust necessary to get your work done.

In America, we tend to share very little about ourselves in the workplace or with our clients. Women are especially guarded about drinking too much with colleagues and revealing certain aspects of their private lives. We are sensitive to our work environment and dress appropriately. In fact, we can be chastised if we appear to be too sexy.

It's obvious that there are different rules in different cultures, and in order to be successful working in a global environment, we need to be mindful of different cultures.

INSEAD professor Erin Meyer, author of *The Culture Map: Breaking through the Invisible Boundaries of Global Business*, says that if your goal is to make it to a high-level position in a global company, then it behooves you to spend a lot of energy learning how to adapt your style to work in different ways. Meyer calls this "authentic flexibility." This means understanding that you are deeply rooted in the culture in which you were raised and that, if you are going to motivate employees or negotiate the best deals with clients in different parts of the world, you need to understand their culture.

Multicultural global teams working virtually have another layer of communication-related complexity. Americans work in a "task-oriented culture" and are therefore more likely to use e-mail more than other cultures. These e-mails can often be misunderstood by other people who are from more "relationship-oriented cultures."

Meyer tells the story of one Russian woman in her seminar who commented, "You know Americans on my team send me these e-mails. And they don't say 'Dear So and So.' They just get right to the content, and then they sign their names with their initials. And I just look at the e-mail and think, 'Don't you even care enough about me to write your name?'"

Because we as Americans are task oriented and respectful of people's time, we think we are showing sensitivity with our direct and abbreviated content. When we sign an e-mail with our initials, we consider it to be informal friendliness.

Meyer offers some very simple rules from the World Bank for virtual communication across cultures. When you write an e-mail, always write, "'Dear So and So.' You always put in two sentences, 'How are you?' or something friendly, and then sign at the end with something like 'Best regards' and then your name." To be honest, Meyer recommends that when you're working internationally, it's always better to pick up the phone and minimize e-mails.

It is critically important as we move into a more global and virtual workplace that we develop a sensitivity to and understanding of other cultures to build relationships of trust. These relationships can be potential sources of information or job opportunities, especially if you work in a global company.

Summary

You've learned that the Pass Go Card helps you get ahead and stay ahead by building a strong network of people who support, protect, and promote you. Without a strategic network behind you, you don't have much political capital. Your Pass Go Card gives you access to information that helps you to avoid political land mines. It offers you the inside scoop on the way decisions are made and how to better position yourself for advancement.

In This Chapter, We Have Learned

- The importance of a strategic network for career advancement and increased income.
- How to identify and map your power network.
- How to make connections and build relationships of trust.
- Paying it forward pays off.

5

The Get Out of Jail Free Card

Sponsorship

I magine this for a minute. Instead of feeling unsure about your future in the company, you suddenly have a clear direction and goal, and someone who supports you every step of the way. This person introduces you to the "right" people in the organization who have power and influence. This person not only suggests that you find high-profile assignments but also makes it happen for you and promotes you, your accomplishments, and your potential. People in the organization automatically respect you because this high-level executive believes in you and has taken you under his or her wing.

You might think this is a pipe dream, but it can be reality when you have a Get Out of Jail Free Card. It's the reality of having a sponsor. Just as the Get Out of Jail Free Card gets you out of tough situations in Monopoly and propels you forward, sponsorship protects you and promotes you to win in the workplace. It's the fast track—the fastest, most powerful way to advance your career. A sponsor paves the way for you to make it to the top. He or she literally pulls you up through the ranks by creating visibility and opportunities.

Sylvia Ann Hewlett, chairman and CEO of the Center for Talent Innovation, has done extensive research on sponsorship. Writing for the *Harvard Business Review Blog Network,* she cites *The Sponsor Effect,* a study by the Center for Work-Life Policy (CWLP), which defines a sponsor "as someone who uses chips on his or her protégé's behalf and advocates for his or her next promotion as well as doing at least two of the following: expanding the perception of what the protégé can do; making connections to senior leaders; promoting his or her visibility; opening up career opportunities; offering advice on appearance and executive presence; making connections outside the company; and giving advice. Mentors proffer friendly advice. Sponsors pull you up to the next level."[1]

I would have loved to have had a sponsor during my corporate career, but I had no idea that this type of support and advocacy even existed. I did, however, frequently consult with mentors from both inside and outside my company when I needed a reality check or advice about my current situation or career. At the time, I didn't refer to them as mentors, but they were people whom I respected and knew would point me in the right direction and let me talk through my current issues.

Mentors versus Sponsors

Let me start by saying that you should have both mentors and sponsors. Both are valuable relationships for supporting your career advancement. You should not choose one over the other. Mentors give you great advice. They are often role models who provide you with sound personal and professional advice based on their own successful experience in business. Most of these relationships are not formal. You might reach out to mentors when you want their input, and they are usually very willing to offer advice and spend time with you. They want you to be successful.

A mentor might be your current or former boss. Early in my career, I looked to my boss, Kathy, as a role model. Kathy was a direct, no-nonsense communicator with a big heart. She was masterful at navigating in a company run by men. They respected her and she never gave up her authenticity to be successful. I learned a lot from observing her in the workplace. Kathy also gave me great advice as a new manager about how to run my territory. I still remember her telling me to hire a team that complements me and to hire to my weakness, and that advice served me well through the years, especially in my CEO role at ServiceMaster. She was invested in my success, but she didn't have the high-level clout of a sponsor who would have actively accelerated my promotion to leadership.

Anisha, who I've mentioned in previous chapters, was originally connected to her mentor through a program at Harvard Business School, and Anisha has consulted with her over the last six years. "She's just been a great sounding board. You know, I call her regularly; we've become friends now, so we chit-chat about our personal lives as well. But over the years, as I'm thinking of making a change, or I'm in a new role, I call her for advice. And right now, I'm very seriously considering taking an external offer. So I was talking to her just yesterday and today, and over the last couple of weeks to get her advice on, 'Is it the right external move?'"

This is a great example of the type of advice a mentor can offer you. But here's the big difference between what a mentor versus a sponsor will do for you. If Anisha had a sponsor, that sponsor would give her advice about her next career move *and* would also help her find that new position. The sponsor would suggest specific companies for Anisha to consider and would make calls to his or her connections to open doors for Anisha. In other words, the sponsor would act on Anisha's `behalf and help Anisha find the best possible new role in a company by speaking to his or her contacts and helping to promote Anisha.

The bottom line is: You need mentors and sponsors. Mentors can be anyone whose opinion you respect. They can be at any level inside or outside the organization. Sponsors, however, are a high-level executives with the power to make things happen for you. They take on a protégé with the specific goal of promoting them to leadership positions. It's a much more powerful relationship because it consists of both advice and action.

PricewaterhouseCoopers LLP has moved from offering mentorship to offering sponsorship programs for high-potential women because sponsorship has a direct impact on advancing women to leadership positions. Bob Moritz, chairman and senior partner of PwC, talks about the difference between mentorship and sponsorship: "A mentor calls a woman into the room and says, 'This is what you should do.' Or, the woman goes into that mentor's room and says, 'What's your advice?' And they give that advice, and typically, it's behind closed doors. And that's fine. But a sponsor has a personal interest in somebody—that is, personally vested—that they are willing to invest their personal capital to make something happen. I'll use the word *disruptive*. And, in that case, a lot of times, they will go out of the way—exert that capital to create an opportunity or make an opportunity become reality. Or, coach people. And at times, that sponsor will do it without the person even knowing it. And it has enabled the success of that person. So again, on the one hand, mentors are a bunch of words and advice. On the other side, the sponsorship is words, advice, and being disruptive; being assertive; being disruptive and actually doing something about it. And that's the analogy between the talk and the action."[2]

It is this disruptive action on your behalf that makes the sponsorship powerful. Remember the biblical story of Moses parting the Red Sea so that his people could cross to the other side? It's a great metaphor for what sponsorship can do for you. It's just that powerful! Sponsors intentionally clear the way for you to get ahead. They purposefully promote you and create highly visible opportunities for you so that your path to leadership is accelerated.

The Importance of Sponsorship for Women

According to *The Sponsor Effect*, sponsorship provides a statistical benefit of up to 30 percent for high-profile assignments, promotions, and pay raises, yet very few women have sponsors.[3] In fact, men are

46 percent more likely than women to have a sponsor.[4] Women are overmentored and undersponsored. As a result, they miss out on the positive impact of having a sponsor.

The report quantifies this impact: "Without a sponsor behind them, 43 percent of men and 36 percent of women will ask their manager for a stretch assignment; with sponsor support, the numbers rise, respectively, to 56 percent and 44 percent."

"The majority of unsponsored men (67 percent) and women (70 percent) resist confronting their boss about a raise; with a sponsor in their corner, nearly half of men and 38 percent of women summon the courage to negotiate."

"A sponsor confers a statistical career benefit of anything from 22 to 30 percent, depending on what's being requested (assignment or pay raise) and who's asking (men or women)."[5]

The report states that there is a direct relationship between a lack of sponsorship opportunities for women and the absence of women in leadership positions.

Most organizations, professions, and communities have been historically dominated by men, and although this is changing, women often face an uphill task when they seek to advance professionally. Without active sponsorship from senior leaders—the majority of whom are male—women will not have the empowerment, exposure, and experience they need for career growth.

This type of support has been available informally to men under the guise of the old boys' club or patronage. Senior male executives are still more likely to sponsor young men who remind them of themselves. But CWLP research confirms that high-potential women need the advocacy and support of sponsors in order to get ahead and stay ahead.

Until now you may not have even been aware that the Get Out of Jail Free card is available for you. As I said before, I had no idea that this type of relationship existed. But now that you know about the power of sponsorship, it needs to be on your radar screen!

The Benefits of Having a Sponsor

Sponsorship is a crucial relationship that can help you to succeed on many levels.

Shaheeda developed a relationship with her sponsor over the course of her career at Microsoft. The woman who is her sponsor has grown significantly in her career and has a great deal of influence. "The one thing that I've noticed that she does—we only talk once in a while, but whenever I'm in a meeting, she actually comes to me and reaches out to me—and either gives me a hug or sort of pats me on my shoulder and chats with me really quickly. And I have noticed when that happens, something changes in people's minds. Suddenly, they start seeing me as someone of value. And people who would be sort of in an adversarial position to what I'm advocating suddenly become believers. It demonstrates to others that I have promise."

That's the subtle power a sponsor can have. Their advocacy gets people's attention. It earns you immediate respect, sometimes just with a public pat on the shoulder!

Similarly, Chris Reilly was amazed at the effect of having lunch in the cafeteria with her sponsor, who was a CEO. She noticed that people started returning her phone calls faster. This was an unexpected side benefit. But her sponsor also exercised his power and influence. "He chose me to be the head of corporate development when Tyco had just bought us. He was putting his political clout on the table and saying, 'I think this girl can do this job.'" Later in her career, another sponsor, also a CEO, put her forward to run one of the divisions of her company.

Katherine says that having a sponsor has been completely transformational for her. In the last 18 to 24 months, she has become more aware of the power of having sponsors, how to manage the relationships, and how to leverage them. Her career has taken off with two promotions during this short time period! Her most recent promotion was the direct result of her strongest sponsor's power and influence.

This opportunity developed in Katherine's business line at the bank, and her sponsor, who had direct oversight over this business, promoted her for the position. "They could have chosen many solutions in terms of how to fill the role. And I know for a fact that he wanted me to be part of that solution. And it was engineered in a way that I could be part of the solution to fill that role. So that was very consciously, from his perspective, wanting to give me an opportunity. He took the view that I had potential and wanted to find a solution that could include me in that solution for this business."

Megan, who we met in Chapter 4, provides more visibility for her protégé, Alison. She actively promotes her across the company. She articulates to the senior people at the firm the value of Alison's role, her value to Megan, and why she should be worth money over time. This advocacy positions Alison for success.

Women and Sponsorship

Are you scratching your head and asking yourself why more women don't have sponsors when this is such a powerful relationship? There are several reasons to consider.

Gender Bias and Stereotypes

Since most organizations are still run by men, subtle gender bias remains a factor. I referred to this earlier when I commented that the Get Out of Jail Free Card has been available informally to men for decades. Male leaders are more likely to see potential in men who are most like themselves.

Also, gender stereotypes associated with leadership roles, though not as obvious, work against women in many organizations, as they are channeled into more supportive positions without P&L responsibility or the same advancement potential as their male colleagues.

What did you observe when you used your Magnifying Glass in Chapter 4? What is the reality about sponsorship in your company? How many high-potential men versus women are being sponsored?

Because sponsors take a risk by publically supporting their protégé, they may also be hesitant to support women, especially women with children. They assume that these women are less available for the C suite and perhaps not as committed as men. Again, this assumption is rooted in gender stereotypes. It's important, therefore, to declare your career goals and your commitment to reaching those goals.

Senior executive men may also be hesitant to sponsor an ambitious young woman because the relationship might be misconstrued as sexual. The man thus might avoid taking such a public risk. Restricting your meetings to work hours and publically announcing the sponsor relationship will help to alleviate any notion of an affair.

Women's Lack of Self-promotion and Visibility

As we discussed in Chapter 2, men are much better at self-promotion and self-advocacy. Women must learn to use the Mirror to identify and communicate their value proposition across the organization so that key stakeholders and potential sponsors understand how they contribute to the success of the business. Without this visibility, women are less likely to be tapped for sponsorship if formal programs exist. If you are seeking a sponsor on your own, you need to build your political and social capital in order to get on a senior executive's radar. You must have a reputation for excellent performance and consistent delivery of results.

Women Don't Know How to Get a Sponsor

Almost every time I speak about the importance of sponsorship for women in a workshop, someone will ask me how to get a sponsor. They want to know how to identify potential sponsors, how to nurture the relationships, and, most importantly, how to ask. I will discuss this in more detail later in the chapter, but it requires you to use all the tools in your Political Toolkit: the Mirror for self-promotion; the Magnifying Glass to understand the unwritten rules, observe the dynamics, and identify potential champions and sponsors; the Pass Go Card to strategically network and build relationships of trust and influence; the Get Out of Jail Free Card to get a sponsor; and the GPS, which is coaching support, to keep you on track and give you ongoing feedback and advice.

Women's Reluctance to Use Relationships to Get Ahead

As we mentioned in Chapter 4, this reluctance to leverage relationships is a huge barrier to women's advancement. Men view relationships differently and use them to their advantage in the workplace. Women feel that using our connections to get ahead and stay ahead is somehow dirty and unethical. If you are lucky enough to be assigned a sponsor or find someone willing to be your sponsor, you need to play that card! That's the surest way to move up quickly. Using your Pass Go Card to build a strong network will help you not only to identify a sponsor but also to build mutually beneficial relationships that can lead to sponsorship.

Women Don't Identify the Right People for Sponsorship

Hewlett says that the only thing that matters when looking for a sponsor is power. Women instinctively go for the wrong person; they tend to go for a leader they want to emulate, a role model: "According to survey data from the Center for Talent Innovation, 49 percent of women in the marzipan layer, that talent-rich band just under the executive level, search for support among someone 'whose leadership style I admire.' What style is that? Forty-two percent are looking for sponsorship from collaborative, inclusive leaders because that style of leadership is one they embody or hope to emulate.

"The problem is, those aren't the leaders with the power to push promising women to the corporate heights. . . . In short, what female talent values and seeks in a sponsor just isn't on offer among those with real power in the organization. This profound mismatch helps explain why so many women—40 percent—fail to find the real deal: sponsors who deliver."[6]

Women Undervalue the Power of Sponsorship

Because many organizations do not have formal sponsorship programs, many women are unaware of the opportunity to work with a sponsor. But even if you are familiar with sponsorship, you may not recognize how compelling this relationship can be for your future. You may still hold on to the belief that your performance alone will help you get ahead.

According to the CWLP, "77 percent of women believe that hard work and long hours, not connections, contribute most to their advancement."[7] We have discussed the importance of using the Pass Go Card to build and leverage relationships. If you are looking for a sponsor, you must network strategically with key stakeholders and people with power and influence.

How to Find a Sponsor

There are two ways to get a sponsor: through a formal sponsorship program or by your individual efforts. Both approaches require the use of the tools in your Political Toolkit.

Company Sponsorship Program

1. Is there a program?

    We used the Magnifying Glass in Chapter 3 to find out if a sponsorship program is available in your company. Use your Pass Go Card to tap into your network. You can certainly ask your colleagues, boss, mentor, or someone in HR if a formal program exists or if sponsors are available.

If you work for a large company, you might find out about your company's programs on such lists as DiversityInc's list of Top 50 Companies for Diversity[8] or Working Mother's annual list of the NAFE (National Association of Female Executives) Top 50 Companies for Executive Women.[9]

2. What are the requirements?

If there is a sponsorship program, get as much information as you can about what it takes to qualify for a sponsor. Get the requirements in writing if possible.

3. What is the process?

Human Resources may tell you the rules about acceptance into a sponsorship program, but what have you identified as the "unwritten rules"?

Stephanie, a coaching client in the health care industry, was given a sponsor through her HR department. "I had applied for a position that I didn't get because I didn't have enough experience, and so they thought having a sponsor would be a very good way to further develop my skills. They assigned one to me based on personality."

Once again, it's time to pull out your Magnifying Glass and Pass Go Card to answer the following questions:

- Who are the decision makers or gatekeepers for these programs?
- Who has to recommend you?
- Who in the company has sponsors?
- Are there women in the program?
- Who endorsed or recommended them?

4. Take action.

Figure out if you meet the qualifications for the program. If you do, then make your case with HR, your boss, or whomever you have determined is the decision maker. Don't forget to use your value proposition for this! If you discover that you have some areas that need improving before you qualify, put a plan in place to fill in the gap.

What have you learned about how women in your company get sponsors? Identify some executives that you know or need to know who can endorse you. You also might consider asking a senior executive with whom you have a relationship if he or she will sponsor you. We will discuss the best approach for this a little later in this chapter. Your Mirror, Magnifying Glass, and Pass Go Card will all help you with this action plan.

Independent Sponsorship

Don't let the fact that your company doesn't have a sponsorship program deter you from finding one on your own. Remember, the Get Out of Jail Free Card is the fastest track to the top, and you should make it your intention as a high-potential professional woman to play this card for your advancement.

So how do you find such a person in your organization? The good news is that you have already done much of the legwork in the previous chapters with your Magnifying Glass and Pass Go Card. Use your Magnifying Glass and Pass Go Card to find the people at a senior level who have the power, and put a strategic plan in place to meet them and build and nurture the relationship.

1. Review your data.

    Who are the people you have identified as having power and influence in the company from Chapter 3? Who are the people, especially women, who have been successful? Do they have sponsors? Who are they? What have these women done to get noticed? Who are their allies and champions?

2. Look at your Power Network.

    Identify a number of potential sponsors. You might begin by asking your boss or HR for advice on possible candidates. They also might help by introducing you to these senior executives.

    Perhaps a former boss who has been promoted is a possible sponsor. Maybe someone who has previously served as a mentor for you or is currently your mentor has the potential to be your sponsor. You might approach this person about his or her willingness to change the nature of the relationship.

Remember, you're looking for an ally and champion, not a friend. You may not admire their leadership style, but it's important that they have power—the real power to change your career. Sylvia Ann Hewlett notes that "would-be sponsors in large organizations are ideally two levels above you with line of sight to your role; in smaller firms, they're either the founder or president or are part of his or her inner circle."[10]

Katherine's relationship with her sponsor grew organically. Ten years ago he hired her, and out of a simple interview grew a relationship. And that's developed through an interaction on the business side. He has followed her career for 10 years and has been an influencer during that time period. Now that he is based in the United States, he has become her strongest sponsor and can actually affect and direct the path of her career.

Davia Temin had a very successful corporate career and is now founder of Temin & Company, a consulting organization. She told me she never set out to find a sponsor. "It just happened because we liked each other and we worked together, and we did some really nifty things, and it came through the work. I think he saw in me something he admired; I was bold, but smart about it. And I seek to be a nice person. I have a wicked sense of humor that I think he liked. And I think, insofar as someone from the opposite sex could remind him of himself, I did."

Most women I've spoken to who have sponsors agree with Katherine and Davia. These relationships develop over time. Potential sponsors need to be aware of your accomplishments. Their trust in you grows as they follow your performance and impact on the business.

3. Make a strategic plan.

   You should now have a list of possible sponsors. Next, refer to your Power Network to determine the strength of your connection with them. In many cases, you may not have any relationship with them. Use your strategic contacts to get introductions if possible. Review the Pass Go Card approach in Chapter 4 for building relationships of trust. Tap into your network for information on what motivates and interests your potential sponsors. Be creative and think of ways to be visible with these people, and showcase your talent and accomplishments. Volunteer for special projects to give you visibility to senior management.

4. Take action.

As you are scheduling your week, make dedicated time to meet targeted individuals for lunch or coffee. In the beginning, you may just be meeting with people who can provide information in hopes of getting introductions. Don't get discouraged. These relationships take time to nurture. Now that you are no longer leaving your career destiny to chance, your continued focus will propel you to act on your plan!

Hewlett recommends having more than one sponsor. The reasoning is that you don't want to put all your eggs in one basket. What happens if your sponsor leaves the company? In that case, you would have to start all over again. "The solution, of course, is to cultivate more than one sponsor, at least in a medium-sized to large firm. In organizations with fewer than 10 people, you're probably best served by having one or two sponsors outside the firm as well as in it, in the same industry. The ideal life raft in larger organizations, CTI research shows, consists of three sponsors: two within your organization, one in your line of sight and one in a different department or division, and one outside your firm. The '2 + 1 Rule,' as we call it, holds true for every career stage, from entry level to executive."[11]

Make Yourself Sponsor Ready

Regardless of our intention to have a sponsor, a sponsor doesn't just show up one day and offer support. According to Sylvia Ann Hewlett,

"Sponsors don't magically appear, like fairy godmothers (or godfathers), to hard-working Cinderellas. Sponsorship must be earned."[12]

So let's talk about what you can do to earn sponsorship.

Be a Rock Star

Consistently great performance is the first necessary requirement for sponsorship. Katherine believes that "at the end of the day, people have to believe in your capabilities. They want to be associated with your success, and they want to be a part of your success."

Not only do you need to have the talent and track record, but also key people in the organization need to know your value proposition. You must use the Mirror, Magnifying Glass, and Pass Go Card to build visibility with the right people. Remember, it is one thing to produce great results, but if no one knows about them, you remain invisible.

Gain Respect and Trust through Hard Work

Demonstrating that you are willing to go the extra mile in terms of your time and energy is critical to gain the respect and trust of your sponsor. Your sponsor needs to be confident that you will follow through and meet and exceed his or her expectations, as your sponsor is actively promoting you and putting his or her career on the line to move yours forward.

One of Megan's sponsors is the CIO and founder of the firm. He recognizes her dedication to the firm and the fact that she works long hours. "I'm working really hard. My boss runs into me in the office on a Sunday, and he tells me, 'You know, you treat this firm like it's your firm already. And I love that. I really respect that. I want to grow more people into partners, and you're behaving like a partner before you're a partner. And I think that's great.'"

Shared Mission or Values

Megan says her sponsors agree with her vision for her role in the company and support her initiatives. They align with the overall direction of the firm. With this common mission, it is understood that her success will benefit the company to reach its goals.

Mutual Benefit

What most people fail to recognize is that the sponsor relationship is beneficial to both the sponsor and protégé. The protégé gets put on the fast track to a leadership position through exposure and promotion. The senior executive benefits through the expansion of his or her reach and impact across the organization. CEOs and top managers acknowledge that they wouldn't be where they were without loyal protégés.[13]

Katherine sees the sponsor relationship as a bilateral one. "If you're someone that they believe in, they want to be seen as your sponsor, because that reflects well on them as well. At least for me, the people who have worked better in terms of being my sponsors are people with whom I have this two-way relationship. I deliver for them, and they make sure that I get the opportunities as well. There's an allegiance that's expected within the firm."

What are some ways you can help your sponsor?

- Information

    Often senior leadership can be isolated and/or fed inaccurate information. A protégé can give them a reality check.

    Stephanie says that her sponsor finds out from her about issues with the leadership team on the ground level. He is insulated by virtue of his high-level position and would never get this information through the normal pathways. He appreciates the real feedback from her about what's going on. She gives an example: "He's been told by senior management in North America that everything is good through the PES, Performance Evaluation System; that all performance evaluations have been completed, and it's all been done. I told him that that hasn't happened. Goals have not been set for me and mine have not been done, even though I've asked repeatedly. And even when he's gone back to ask, he's been told, 'No, everybody's done, it's fine.' So he's seeing that there's a disconnect between what's actually happening and what he's been told."

When Chris Reilly came home from business trips, she would relate important information, especially the type of information that she knew her sponsor cared about. After one trip, for example, she let him know that when she pulled up to the company's international headquarters in Dublin, the sign over the door still said Dell, not CIT.

She also informed him that Dublin was on a different e-mail system. They were still on Dell's system and apparently had built some sort of bridge between that one and CIT's. It delayed e-mails significantly. Chris was still in the office with her sponsor as he picked up the phone to call someone in IT to verify this and charge him with fixing the e-mail system immediately.

- Expertise

  Another example of how you can help your sponsor is by offering your expertise in an area where they might be lacking knowledge—for instance, social media or technology. Younger protégés are likely to be more adept in this area than senior executives.

- Favors

  Katherine says, "Sponsors put their reputation on the line for you and they expect you also to take up projects when they ask you to." She has taken on special projects for her sponsors. Her main sponsor in New York asked her to assume leadership of the women's initiative at the bank. He is the lead executive sponsor of this organization; he is very passionate about it and is committed to take it to next level. He knows he can count on Katherine to do just that.

Framing the Relationship

Corporate sponsorship programs will most likely provide specific goals and expectations for both sponsor and protégé. Many companies track results to make sure the sponsor relationship is working for both parties and also to document the efficacy of the program. Your company may, in fact, monitor results by gender if they have a corporate goal to increase the number of women in leadership roles, as sponsorship is a key initiative to support this goal.

If you are in a corporate program or if you have secured your own sponsor, you should meet with the sponsor early on to establish some ground rules and expectations. Going over the formal guidelines of a corporate initiative or setting your own mutually agreed-upon goals and time frames is a great way to begin a relationship of accountability. This exercise will benefit both parties.

Having a discussion about what your sponsor expects in terms of frequency of meetings or communication and the type of communication (phone, e-mail, text, video chat) is important. Setting an agenda for your meetings will help you prepare and stay focused. Establishing expectations around performance is also recommended.

As with any action plan, the place to start is with your career goal. Let your sponsor know your goal and get some initial agreement on whether this is viable given your talent and experience. You will want to solicit his or her feedback, not only on the goal, but also on realistic time frames for reaching it. Getting the sponsor's initial buy-in is critical. Also, the more specific you can be about your objectives, the easier it will be for your sponsor to help you by creating opportunities and providing introductions to the right people. Your sponsor may even suggest a different direction based on what he or she knows about you and potential opportunities in the firm.

What should be your focus over the next designated time period? Again, getting specifics is helpful. Davia says she met with her sponsor quarterly, and he gave her a list of things to do. She did her best to check off everything on this list before they met again. Sharing your upcoming calendar and asking for input is also a good idea.

Part of the ongoing conversation should always be about how you can help your sponsor. Are there special projects where you should be involved? What type of information can you provide to the sponsor, as we discussed with Stephanie, Chris, and Katherine.

It is understood that you will demonstrate loyalty and support your sponsor's initiatives in the company. Ask if there are any current or upcoming efforts that should be on your radar screen.

Summary

You've learned the power of using the Get Out of Jail Free Card for sponsorship. This is, by far, the fastest track to the top, but it does require all the tools in your Political Toolkit to identify and secure a sponsor, and develop a mutually beneficial relationship. The Mirror helps you to promote your accomplishments and potential; to build visibility and credibility. The Magnifying Glass focuses your attention on the workplace dynamics to understand the rules, as well as the unwritten rules, for getting a sponsor; to uncover who has power and influence and can assist you in reaching your career goal. The Pass Go Card helps you to build a network of potential mentors and sponsors and begin building relationships of trust. And the Get Out of Jail Free Card shows you how to find and get a sponsor.

In This Chapter, We've Learned

- The definition of the sponsor relationship.
- The difference between a mentor and a sponsor.
- The benefits of sponsorship for your career.
- What holds women back from getting sponsors.
- How to make yourself ready for the sponsor.
- How to frame the sponsor relationship to set expectations and time frames.

6

The GPS

Executive Coaching

first met Katherine two years ago when she attended a workshop I
was facilitating for the Athena Center for Leadership at Barnard
College. At the time, I recognized her to be an ambitious and talented
woman, but she was frustrated with her lack of promotion and
visibility at the bank where she worked. Over the course of the
two days, it became clear to Katherine that she was not thinking
strategically about her career. "I really never thought about coaching
before then, and I realized that I needed to manage my career the same
way that I managed my business. And I guess I'm stereotyping a little
bit, but in usual female fashion, you think that if you keep your head
down and do a good job, people will notice. It doesn't always happen.
And that was a big realization for me. I actually do need to take
control of my career. I'd been planning my jobs, my path, my
technical expertise, and my skill set. But what I had not been doing
was planning my career and managing my political connectivity
within the firm. And I haven't been managing all of the formal and
informal decision-making processes that would get me to where I
wanted to be."

Katherine hired me as her coach following that workshop, and within the first six months, she was promoted to managing director. Within the next year, she was promoted to be the co-head of the Financial Institutions Group, North America, Global Banking and Markets.

How did that happen? Katherine had everything it took to be successful before she hired me, but she didn't have a GPS for her career, which is coaching support.

What Is Coaching?

When I started coaching in 2006, many people didn't understand what coaching was. They were familiar with coaching in sports, but the idea that you could have a coach help your business or career was pretty far-fetched. In the last decade, coaching has become widely accepted as a profession. In fact, you can find coaches to help you with almost any personal or professional issue.

In sports, a coach provides the guidance to improve your performance and be the best you can be. The coach offers support and practical tips on how to step up your game. The same is true of an executive coach.

An executive coach is your partner in helping you reach your goals and your full potential. In this case, the game is business. And as a player in this game, you need to understand the playing field, the players, the rules, and what it takes to win. Your coach shows you what it takes to be at the top of your game and gives you tips on how to score points with the eventual goal of crossing the finish line a winner.

A good coach honors your agenda as a top priority. As your partner, the coach is completely focused on helping you be successful according to what you believe success to be. The coach respects where you are in your journey and gives his or her best guidance and support without judgment.

Given the complexities of the work environment today, coaching is extremely beneficial for anyone trying to navigate to the top. It gives you an extra advantage. Through the coaching process, you are learning about yourself, your organization, and the optimal way to position yourself to get ahead.

The International Coach Federation, which is the only accrediting organization for coaching, defines coaching as "partnering with clients in a thought-provoking and creative process that inspires them to maximize their personal and professional potential, which is particularly important in today's uncertain and complex environment."[1]

An excellent way to maximize your career potential is to have the guidance and constructive feedback from an executive coach—your GPS. There are a variety of ways you can work with a coach to get this special support.

Different Types of Executive Coaching

The best way to begin the process of looking for a coach is to define your career goal. What are your ambitions? What are your time frames? What type of support do you need to reach your goal? Once you start searching for a coach, you will discover there are coaches who specialize in certain areas. For instance, there are career transition coaches, presentation coaches, leadership coaches, and communication coaches as well as general executive coaches. You may also want to consider if it's important for you to work with a coach who specializes in helping professional women. Do you prefer a male or female coach?

Personally, I looked for different types of coaching support at different stages of building my business that were dependent on my needs at the time. The bottom line is that there is a variety of coaching support available, so it's best to start with your own goals and narrow down the type of help you need. From there, you can find the best coach or coaching program to support you moving forward.

I begin my coaching engagements with an exploratory call. This usually comes in the form of a complimentary 30-minute session. This session is especially helpful for me as well as the prospective client. The prospective client can assess whether or not they want to work with me and if my approach and style match their needs. From the coaching perspective, I evaluate what the major challenges are and make a recommendation for ongoing support.

Coaching support is available through individualized programs (in person, or via phone or Skype); group programs (online, via phone, or in person); VIP Days (in-person or virtual full- or half-day individualized support); mastermind groups (live or virtual groups with similar interests and goals who work collaboratively with each other and their coach); and workshops, seminars, and conferences. You may wish to start with a group to get the experience of coaching and then move to a more customized individual program that is optimal. It depends on your comfort level, time frame, and budget.

Before I make any recommendations for programs, I ask potential clients their goals and time frames. Some programs, such as my full-day VIP Day or the premium six-month program, offer intense interaction and therefore support more aggressive time frames. In fact, the six-month premium program, which provides feedback from a choice of five colleagues and supervisors, along with twelve 60-minute coaching sessions, is the most successful and therefore most popular program I offer for women who want to advance quickly. Every woman who has enrolled in this program has been promoted within one year!

Regardless of the program, I always begin the coaching process with a 90-minute strategy session. Once clients have formally engaged and signed a contract, I send them an in-depth questionnaire. The information from the clients' responses provides the starting point for this session. We spend time discussing their background and experience, but pay special attention to the current work situation and what challenges there are relative to getting ahead in this environment.

I ask clients what they like best about their job. What do they like least about it? This helps me determine if their job is a good fit. I ask them to describe the company culture and their relationship with their boss. If they rate the relationship with their boss as fair or poor, what would it take to improve it? And most important, I ask them what they believe their potential is for being promoted in their present organization. Understanding the workplace dynamics is critical for me to provide the best possible advice and support.

During this initial session, the clients refine their career goal, and we jointly establish realistic goals for the coaching work. Each subsequent session supports both sets of goals. Although revisiting the goals may become necessary due to unforeseen circumstances, I keep my clients on track for whatever they have initially declared as their goal. That is the career GPS!

The Importance of a Career GPS for Women

Let's talk about the GPS. The Global Positioning Satellite system, or GPS, has become an indispensable tool in our everyday lives. With our handy GPS, we don't have to worry about how to reach our destination. The GPS guides us there with step-by-step instructions. It's actually comforting to know that there is a satellite up there somewhere that knows where we are and how to get where we want to go. Before the GPS, I remember that preparing for a business trip included printing out directions from the airport to the hotel, trying to read the directions while driving, and sometimes being led to the wrong location! It was not only frustrating but also scary at times. If you took a wrong turn, you literally were lost. There was no recalculation; no one there to help you get back on track. Executive coaching, the career GPS, provides the same type of support and direction.

This guidance is especially important for women because their journey to leadership is not direct; they encounter many obstacles and unexpected changes along the way. Savvy and ambitious women recognize the value of executive coaching and rely on a GPS to help them get ahead and stay ahead.

Though we still refer to the notion of "climbing a corporate ladder" to advance our careers, the concept of a ladder is not realistic for women in today's workplace. Authors Alice H. Eagly and Linda L. Carli describe women's career path as a labyrinth, "which captures the varied challenges confronting women as they travel, often on indirect paths, sometimes through alien territory, on their way to leadership."[2]

There isn't necessarily a direct path to the top for women. If that were true, we could make a concrete plan and the next step up would always be a logical move. But our careers don't always progress logically one step up at a time. We must constantly "recalculate" and reassess our next move, and it takes savvy and strategy. I refer to women's advancement to leadership as more of a glass grid, because while it's true that we need to negotiate around barriers, as in a labyrinth, the politics, subtle gender bias, and many of the obstacles we encounter are not obvious to us until we literally bump into them or get blindsided. This is the case for having coaching support to guide you, the GPS tool.

Authors Pamela L. Perrewé and Debra L. Nelson address the need for women to work with an executive coach because of the special challenges women face in the workplace. They state that "the focus of executive coaching is usually on skills such as political savvy and strategic vision."[3]

They go on to say, "If women do not embrace the notion that political skill is a necessity for success, there will be fewer women executives. The unique problems that women managers face can be addressed with an individually tailored approach, as offered by executive coaching. Executive coaching increases psychological and social awareness and understanding, as well as the ability to develop and maintain effective interpersonal relationships. These areas are central to the conceptualization of political skill."

In her May 2012 white paper, "Coaching Women in Leadership or Coaching Women Leaders? Understanding the Importance of Gender and Professional Identity Formation in Executive Coaching for Women," the author, Suzette Skinner, recommends that executive coaching support be customized for women due to gender issues.

"She refers to research where female participants were asked what they needed in terms of coaching support. "The key focus areas nominated by participants included confidence building, communication, self-promotion and networking skills, navigating a path toward promotion and managing career transitions."[4]

Because women not only deal with gender issues in the workplace but also have their own internal issues around self-advocacy, networking, and politics, a GPS is essential for career success. Coaching, their career GPS, enhances the effectiveness of all the other tools in the Political Toolkit. It helps them overcome their challenges as a high-achieving woman in a competitive, often male-dominated work environment. Coaching support positions them to reach their full potential.

How the GPS Works with the Other Tools in the Political Toolkit

The GPS and the Mirror

We talked extensively in Chapter 2 about the importance of understanding our value proposition in order to build visibility and gain access to informal networks of power and influence. Yet the process of identifying our value proposition is not an easy one. We often don't comprehend how we uniquely contribute to business outcomes. We get caught up describing ourselves in clichés: We're organized, we're a team player, and we work hard. These overused and generic descriptors do not help us promote ourselves in the workplace. The insightful questioning from a coach guides us through this process of self-discovery to create a powerful value proposition that accurately depicts our contribution to the business and positions us as someone with both talent and potential.

Like many of my other clients, Mary, an associate general counsel at a California hospital system, secured a new position and was promoted because my unique coaching process begins with helping clients like her identify their value proposition. She says, "I found the coaching to be very helpful in my self-examination and reflection. It helped me to articulate my value proposition and clarify my career goals. And as a result of that, I found a new position, and that was a promotion and a challenge for me."

Your career plan follows this important first step. All activities around self-promotion, networking, building visibility and credibility, and seeking sponsorship are based on the ability to understand and then articulate to key stakeholders how you contribute to the business. I can honestly tell you that my clients would not have received promotions if this critical part of the coaching was missing, and it takes the skill of an experienced coach to take you through this exercise. So the GPS, your coach, along with the Mirror, is a powerful first step in your quest to get ahead.

The GPS and the Magnifying Glass

Because our default behavior is to keep our head down and focus on our work, we miss the obvious and subtle politics at play: politics that can derail us if we aren't paying attention. It requires our focused effort to look beyond our desk and gather important information that impacts our careers. A coach helps us to focus on our surroundings and provides guidelines of what to look for to simplify the process.

For me to coach my clients, I need as much information as possible about the culture and dynamics of the organization. How else can I help them navigate? My work with clients helps them not only gather the necessary information but also to objectively assess the political landscape, and together we determine the best plan to move ahead.

In Chapter 3 we used the Magnifying Glass to observe the workplace dynamics; to uncover the rules, unwritten rules, and the politics; and to identify the people with power and influence. The process resulted in the accumulation of a lot of important information. The GPS, your coach, assists you in analyzing the information and turning it into an action plan. This plan shows you how to navigate the realities of your current situation and work environment.

The GPS and the Pass Go Card

Once you have accumulated all the information about the people in your organization who have power and influence over your career, how do you use the Pass Go Card to create your power network? I work with my clients to rank their contacts by influence and prioritize their networking activity. I encourage them to stretch outside their comfort zone and build a network that supports their career goal, not necessarily a network of people they already know and like. I also help my clients manage their time and hold them accountable for actively networking inside and outside the workplace.

Many of my clients don't network strategically. They may or may not understand the importance of networking, but they often don't take the time to nurture and build relationships of trust. In some cases, they don't know where to begin to initiate a new relationship. And the majority of women that I work with at all levels are very hesitant to leverage relationships for quid pro quo. Without the support of a coach, many women will default to their behavior of doing favors over and over again for others without cashing in their chips, and as a result, they lose out on many fortuitous opportunities. This is an area where I urge my clients to step out of their comfort zone and build mutually beneficial relationships.

The GPS and the Get Out of Jail Free Card

We've talked about the Get Out of Jail Free Card as the most powerful political move you can make. Sponsorship is the fastest track to the top. That being said, it's not easy to find a sponsor or the right sponsor. As we discussed in Chapter 5, often women will look for role models who don't have the clout to push them ahead. The GPS, your coach, will assist you in evaluating appropriate sponsors and building mutually beneficial relationships. They will help you manage the relationship for maximum exposure.

I assist my clients with the process of identifying the right sponsor and establishing a framework for the relationship. If your organization has a formal sponsorship program, I work with you to create a plan to be identified as a high-potential employee deserving of sponsorship. Once clients understand the requirements for acceptance into a corporate sponsorship program, we create a plan to bridge the gap between where they are and where they need to be so that they will be selected for this special program.

Because sponsorship is so important, the effort to get sponsors is an ongoing topic for discussion.

How Coaching Helps

The Korn/Ferry Institute, the research and analytics arm of executive recruitment firm Korn/Ferry International, researched the effectiveness of executive coaching. Their findings support the efficacy of coaching to modify behavior and build leadership skills:

- "96 percent of organizations report to have seen individual performance improve since coaching was introduced. Nearly as many (92 percent) also have seen improvements in leadership and management effectiveness."
- "70.7 to 93.8 percent have positive responses, suggesting that coaching contributes to sustained behavioral change."

Executive coaching provides an advantage for high-achieving men and women to advance to leadership roles and be more successful leaders. But, as a professional woman, when you have the support of a customized coaching program that addresses your specific challenges in a male-dominated workplace, you accelerate your professional growth and the attainment of your goal to get ahead.

It is my experience coaching women that there are some fairly common issues that hold women back from reaching their potential. Here are some specific ways coaching supports women to get ahead and stay ahead.

Thinking Strategically about Your Career

We know that women's belief that their hard work and talent alone will get them ahead holds them back. Because many women focus on their jobs and the tasks at hand, they spend little, if any, time planning the direction of their career and evaluating the best path to reach their goals.

When I first started working with Katherine, she was working extremely hard. She had an overwhelming to-do list, and getting everything done was a source of stress. She was going a mile a minute.

In our initial sessions, I suggested to Katherine that she set aside some dedicated time each week to unplug and let go of her tasks. This time allowed her to think about the bigger picture and adopt a more creative approach to her work and career. We identified that the best time for her to do this was during her commute to and from work. She set the intention of doing this, and I held her accountable for creating this free space each week.

Katherine said this was a game changer for her. "I don't think people spend enough time doing this. People should set aside half an hour a week. It's not too much to ask to actually focus on their next steps and what they should be trying to do to get to their next role in their career. People don't do that enough."

Katherine recognizes that setting this time aside to review her week's activities and think about how to approach the next week is invaluable. It is a habit that has helped her escape her daily to-do list and tasks at hand and transition from being a doer to a leader. It was the beginning of a strategic plan that resulted in her two promotions.

Without accountability to a coach, our default behavior is to fill our time with tasks. We need to recognize this and make it our intention to escape from our to-do lists on a regular basis to see the bigger picture for our career. Filling our calendar and scheduling every minute to the max does not help us move forward. It keeps us stuck right where we are. Our best ideas come to us when we slow down.

Accountability

A good coach will hold you accountable for agreed-upon action steps. This is especially important for women who are already juggling many different roles and responsibilities. Often our agendas get lost in the "busyness" of our personal and professional lives. We create goals for ourselves and then lose our focus over time. This is where the rubber meets the road! How serious are you about advancing your career? Are you willing to do the work to get there? I often give my clients assignments between sessions to deepen the work and keep the momentum going.

If you are serious about your ambitions but keep putting them on the back burner, this is an essential reason to hire a coach. Because most of my clients are ambitious high achievers, they are almost always willing to take on any work that will help them get ahead. But I also recognize that their ambitions can sometimes take a back seat to their job and family responsibilities. It is my responsibility as their coach to hold them accountable for agreed-upon action items and remind them of the importance of doing the work in order to reach their goals. If they do the work, they will see the benefits in their career trajectory.

Clarifying Career Goals

I can't tell you how many times I speak with prospective clients about coaching and discover that they want to get promoted and move up, but they don't really know what moving up looks like. They don't have a specific goal in mind, and they don't have a plan beyond doing good work. The GPS is most effective when you have a clear destination. That destination sets the course for your navigation plan to advancement.

Mary found the new strategic focus from our coaching especially helpful. When she took the time to step outside her job responsibilities and think more about where she wanted to go with her career, it became obvious that she needed to make a change in order to achieve her goal. Our work together helped her clarify that her goal to be general counsel of a health care organization could not be realized in her present organization. She started to look for new opportunities that aligned with that goal. "I was able to think more strategically about my career and start opening a job search." That job search resulted in a higher-level position in another hospital that is a stepping-stone for her to reach her long-term goal.

I work with my clients to identify a specific short-term and/or long-term goal so that they can define a clear path to success, evaluate present and future opportunities, and move their careers forward.

Creating a Concrete Action Plan

The GPS is a necessary tool for creating a career plan. You know there are many twists and turns in your path to promotion. Once you have a definitive destination and direction, it's easy to evaluate opportunities that arise or figure out how to overcome any unplanned situations that have the potential to derail you temporarily. With a plan in place, you are better able to "recalculate" and get back on track. Without a plan, you can get so sidetracked that your career goal may never be attained.

Your coach will help you to create SMART goals (Specific, Measurable, Accountable, Realistic, Time bound) and will hold you accountable for the action steps in the plan.

From the onset, Katherine had a very clear long-term goal. Feedback from her colleagues and stakeholders indicated that Katherine was recognized as a top performer but was not viewed in the organization as a leader. We needed to change that perception.

I started by coaching Katherine to think more strategically about where she was headed and how she could reach her goal. Based on the feedback we received, along with Katherine's recognition of her own challenges, we put a strategic plan in place to bridge the gap from being a top performer to being recognized as a leader. Katherine found working her plan to be transformational for her. "It helped me manage my career in a very objective way that was almost like project managed or task oriented. And that's when I started to see results."

Some action items in Katherine's plan were fairly easy to achieve. We learned from the feedback we received that she needed to look like the leader she wanted to become. She acted on this feedback immediately and paid special attention to her wardrobe and appearance. We also received feedback that she needed to slow down a bit, and that included her speech and communications to others so that she wouldn't always appear rushed and stressed. One of the most important things we discussed, however, was how to move Katherine from being a doer to a leader, and that involved her delegating more to her team. Katherine was committed to making the changes, believing that they would help her get promoted, and her hard work paid off within the first six months.

Most of my clients appreciate having the structure of an action plan. With everything else on their plates, they know that they won't lose focus and that if they do the assigned work from our coaching, they will accomplish their goals. Diane, who we met earlier in Chapter 1, thought that having effective strategies of everyday implementation was especially helpful and that working with a coach forced her to "do the work."

Increasing Self-Awareness

Understanding who you are is critical for your career advancement. Self-awareness helps you get ahead. As you learn more about yourself, you see how to leverage your strengths and what behaviors you may need to change to reach your potential. Self-awareness also helps you stay ahead and maintain your status. Your willingness to examine not only your behavior but also how you lead and manage others helps you be more effective over time.

In her book, *Take the Lead,* Betsy Myers writes, "Leadership isn't something you can put on like a suit of clothes or generate by copying someone else. Leadership is about who you genuinely are. Successful leaders are those who are conscious of their behavior and the impact it has on the people around them. These people are willing to step back from the fray and get an accurate picture of what is working in their organizations and what is not. Moreover, they want to know the why. They are willing to examine what behaviors of their own may be getting in the way."[5]

This self-awareness is a reality check that is not easily accomplished without the honest, objective feedback of a good coach. Sometimes clients will come to me after being passed over for a promotion. They feel betrayed and angry. They deserved the promotion. Believe me—I understand that feeling very well, as I was there myself at one point in my career. But often there are important factors that contributed to not receiving the promotion that need to be examined. This is where the hard work comes in.

First, I help my clients in this situation let go of the anger and shift their mind-set from being a victim to taking responsibility for their actions and behavior. They need a reality check, and it's important to learn from the experience. The work of self-discovery is not possible if they are feeling sorry for themselves.

We look very closely at the circumstances. What reason were they given for not receiving the promotion? Is this the real reason? What else can they find out? How was the decision made? Who made it? Who influenced it? Were there politics involved?

Next, we examine if they met all the requirements for the position. Assuming they did, what else was necessary to get the job? Did they have relationships with the decision maker and his or her influencers? Did they create visibility for themselves? Were the right people aware of their value proposition?

At the end of this process, my clients learn a great deal about themselves and begin to see that they, in fact, had some responsibility for not getting the job. Yes, they were qualified, but perhaps another person was chosen because that person was better at working relationships and self-promotion. Now the real work begins! Accepting responsibility prepares you to take action to modify your behavior and do what it takes to get promoted.

Self-awareness is a necessity for advancement. I incorporate exercises and processes to help my clients with this. With my premium coaching program, I solicit feedback from key people in their organization through custom questionnaires and in-depth telephone conversations. Many coaches provide assessments or use the information that human resources provides from any assessments done through your company, such as the Myers-Briggs Type Indicator and DiSC® personality assessment tools, and 360-degree feedback evaluations. The information from these assessments is incorporated into your work with the coach and becomes part of your ongoing action plan.

Overcoming Self-Imposed Barriers

Working with a coach helps you to identify some of the internal barriers that prevent you from reaching your full potential. As we have discussed, many of these internal barriers, such as negative self-talk and limiting beliefs around self-promotion, office politics, and networking, continually sabotage us. We don't believe we are competent. We hold on to the limiting belief that we need to be perfect, and we don't feel qualified to speak up and offer opinions. Our hesitancy to advocate for ourselves and our discomfort with networking limits our visibility in the company. Our avoidance of politics sets us up to be blindsided and overlooked.

Understanding these internal barriers comes from self-reflection and is the key to getting unstuck and moving your career forward. Many women recognize that something is holding them back from realizing their goals, but they may not be able to identify specifics.

I help my clients to embrace these internal barriers and work with them to overcome their limiting beliefs through affirmations and repetitive exercises to break the habit and default thinking.

My client, Lisa, who we have discussed in previous chapters, knew that she was sabotaging herself but needed some help identifying her barriers. This is a fairly common theme that I see with my clients. They are extremely talented overachievers, but something is holding them back from being more successful. They don't always know what that is. Lisa hired me as her coach because she was frustrated with her lack of progress and couldn't figure out on her own what was happening. "I believed I had more potential than where my career was taking me. I could not understand what was holding me back, and looking at other people, I thought, 'You know what? I should be more successful than I am,' and I wanted to pinpoint and figure out why I wasn't actually living up to the potential I thought I had."

Through our conversations, we identified that Lisa had a confidence issue and that her lack of confidence manifested itself in ways that sabotaged her leadership and reputation. It was a classic case of the "Imposter Syndrome" that many women face. Despite their obvious talent, they don't feel as competent as everyone else. They fear that others will find out they aren't smart enough or accomplished enough for their position.

How does this manifest itself? Lisa would overapologize and often start conversations or e-mails with an apology. The constant apologies resulted in her losing power and influence. This behavior put her in a subservient position to others and sabotaged her leadership. Her assumption that she was not competent caused her to second-guess herself. Her hesitancy to speak up and offer opinions had tainted the way others perceived her in the workplace. She wasn't viewed as a strong leader. It was a self-fulfilling prophecy!

She says, "I told myself I am an imposter, and then I'd watch everybody else get all the better jobs. And that happened to me at UBS. I was one of the first people in the department. I had really good backing from all these people, and I just let myself fade away because I always second-guessed myself. I was always apologizing. And then, when I made mistakes, I would second-guess myself more."

Lisa was able to identify the internal dialogue that was holding her back. With the help of exercises and feedback from my coaching, she was able to build her self-awareness around this issue and strengthen her confidence. Coaching gave her the tools to make the necessary changes to overcome her internal barriers and negative self-talk. "When I do go off track, I catch myself and say, 'Okay, what did my coach tell me to do?' And particularly with the 'I'm sorry.' I actually delete it from my e-mails."

As for second-guessing herself, Lisa says, "You know what? My answers may be wrong, but I have to speak up and I have to adjust this issue. All this was because of coaching and not saying 'I'm sorry' and not hanging my head. And those small words from my coach, the small things that resonate through the coaching process actually resonated with me internally and had a knock-on effect in the way I deal with the business world."

Managing the Politics

If office politics is something you avoid, a coach will show you how to assess the workplace dynamics and engage in positive relationship building. It may be necessary to start by shifting your mind-set about politics. A coach can assist you in working through this change in attitude.

The feedback Mary received from clients and supervisors as part of her coaching program was instrumental in creating a plan to help her manage the politics. From the onset, it was obvious that Mary needed to build and nurture relationships in order to get promoted. This was not her comfort zone, but she was willing to do the work, understanding how important it was for her to reach her goal.

Mary says, "I've always been the type of person who tried to avoid politics and kind of looked at that negatively. And so, coaching gave me a different perspective on that and helped me to realize that office politics is really just building relationships within your work environment, and putting it in that different perspective made it more meaningful and easier for me."

We structured a plan to build her internal network. We identified the people whom she needed to get to know better and who needed to know her better, and we prioritized the relationships that needed to be mended and nurtured. From there, Mary's action items each week were to schedule meetings with these people and begin the process of strengthening her network. In the process, Mary was able to create more visibility for herself across her health care system. She volunteered for special projects and, in doing so, built a reputation as someone with leadership potential.

Because women are often intimidated and sabotaged by the politics, it is extremely helpful to hire a coach who can help you understand workplace dynamics. Becky, a Harvard Business School alumni with high potential, looked for a coach who could give her a landscape view of an organization "because I felt that some of my blind spots were the looking up, looking around. You know you can be heads down at work and not see certain things in the workplace. One of the things she and I talked about was that you need to look up. And you need to look around, and you need to build the relationships at your peer level as well as your boss's level. That was my key learning: just observing the environment." Without her coach's guidance, Becky would be challenged to accurately assess how to best move her career forward.

Managing workplace politics is a necessary part of your career advancement, and it is therefore a significant reason to work with a coach. A coach will help you navigate through all the dynamics, including subtle gender issues and difficult relationships.

Working through Challenging Relationships

It is not uncommon for different people to have clashing opinions and beliefs about the way things should happen at work. Sometimes these differences escalate to the point that they cause uncomfortable confrontation. It is therefore of paramount importance that you learn to manage these situations, no matter how challenging, and that you release any emotions that can fuel a large-scale episode. A coach will help you to see these situations objectively and to better understand another's point of view.

Mona says coaching helped her address conflict in the workplace. As a result, she was better equipped to manage her emotional reactions to staff in difficult situations and detach when responding in writing or in person. She was able to maintain her professionalism. As we discussed in Chapter 3, appearing too emotional in the workplace is something that women must be conscious of in order to be considered leadership material.

Mary was having difficulty with a colleague at work. She didn't report to him, but he was in a senior position to her, and so he had influence over her work. "He had a different perspective on an issue we were dealing with, and I didn't agree with his perspective. When I articulated my disagreement, he was not being collaborative and was telling people that I wasn't being collaborative. And so, we were loggerheads, I guess. My coach helped me to put it in perspective. She asked some really good questions that made me reflect on how I was responding and encouraged me to set up a meeting with that person and try to clear the air, and start fresh in a more collaborative way. And it worked."

Creating a Plan for Increasing Your Visibility in the Organization

Visibility is critical for advancement, yet many women don't know where to begin to build their reputation in the company. In Chapter 4, we created a power network and discussed how to build and nurture relationships of trust. A coach will help you identify a realistic plan to reach out to your contacts. A coach will work with you to help you understand how to use your value proposition to leverage relationships with the right people.

The best example of how a coach can support and guide you through this process is that of my client, Katie, who I described in Chapters 1 and 2. Together we developed a game plan to build her visibility. We identified key stakeholders across the company, and Katie met with each of them to get a better understanding of what their business challenges were. She then offered to help them find a technology platform to resolve their challenges. The result was she gained visibility and credibility across the organization. She built a reputation as a subject matter expert who was willing to help the business meet its objectives.

I use this strategic approach with all of my clients who are seeking promotions at their current company. It starts with the work to identify your value proposition and then involves a systematic effort to build a network and communicate how you add value to the business. As we discussed in Chapter 2 with the Mirror, your value proposition positions you as someone with both talent and potential—two necessary ingredients for a promotion.

Strengthening Leadership Skills

During my initial coaching assessment, gaps in skill set and experience are identified. This serves as the foundation for your plan to gain more expertise in preparation for your next role. Remember how we used the Bridging the Gap worksheet in Chapter 3 to outline what you needed to accomplish to meet your goal? As a coach, based on this exercise, I help you find the resources and provide you with the tools to fill the gap.

Many of my clients are top performers, but they are more "doers" than leaders. This seems to be a common theme for high-achieving women. They work really hard and are often hesitant to trust their team to take on more responsibility. The result is they are overwhelmed by their workload and drowning in their tasks. They can't possibly take on any more responsibility. Can you identify with this? Not only are they stressed, but also they are not perceived in the organization as having leadership potential, and this sabotages their efforts to get ahead.

The feedback we received about Katherine identified that to get promoted, she needed to become less of a doer and more of a leader. How to do that? Early in our work together, we focused on the necessity for her to delegate and empower her team. It was obvious that she had to let go in order to move up. Delegating is a win-win situation because as your team becomes more experienced, they will be better able to support you going forward. It also helps position them for future promotions. During our initial sessions, I would challenge Katherine to delegate more. In the beginning, delegation requires you to coach your team members and give them clear direction to ensure that they are set up to be successful. But it's time well spent. In Katherine's case, her team has stepped up to the plate as a result of her trust and guidance, and she has received two promotions within 18 months.

In addition, the feedback from colleagues and supervisors is extremely helpful to fine-tune action plans around leadership. Through questionnaires and telephone interviews, I solicit specific feedback about my clients regarding their executive presence, whether or not they are viewed as having leadership potential, how influential they are, how visible across the organization. It helps me to evaluate their communication skills as well. This feedback is critical for their career advancement plan.

Mona hired a coach when she was promoted to a new role at work. "I understood that I would be working with high-level officials and in areas that I was not comfortable with, supervising more staff and also planning to do new work that would be a different model and approach than had been tried before." Mona's coach was "truly instrumental in helping her continue to be recognized as a leader in the agency."

Coaching helped Lisa take on her new leadership role with confidence. "I came in here with such a different attitude and thinking, I am the leader, and I'm not going to act like everyone's smarter than me and I shouldn't tell them what to do. Coaching helped me to understand that I have the authority and smarts to be able to do this. And that was my job. I'm supposed to act like a leader.

"I kicked butt in a meeting today with my boss about a mistake that happened in my department. And we had some pretty senior leaders on the call. I knew I was going to get my head handed to me. But I sat right up, and I didn't say I was sorry. I just talked about the facts, and I moved on. And then everyone said, 'Oh yeah, to Lisa's point.' Or 'Good point, Lisa.' Or "Great question, Lisa.' And I sat there in amazement. Inside of me, I said, 'Wow, I just spoke up,' because years ago before coaching, I would listen to the other people ask the same questions I wanted to or say the same things I wanted to, and I would say, 'I was just going to say that.' Or, 'That was just in my head,' but I would never speak up. So it's this huge difference, and that has everything to do with coaching." As a result of coaching, Lisa is successfully establishing herself as a strong leader.

Career Transition

If you are feeling stuck and unfulfilled in your current role, or perhaps you have been let go and are forced to make a change, hiring a coach is extremely beneficial for helping you determine the next move and your approach to find a new job in a strategic and logical manner.

The coaching GPS tool provides an objective, nonjudgmental point of view. Clients gain clarity and a new direction from coaching. Both Mary and Lisa say they would still be stuck in their old jobs had it not been for coaching. They worked with me through the job search process as well as interviewing.

Mary had been in the same position as senior counsel at a large California hospital system for 10 years when I met her at a conference a couple of years ago. After discussing her situation in detail, we determined together that she was in a dead-end job with little opportunity for advancement. Mary agreed that the next best step for her was to look outside her organization for another job.

When Mary was going through the interview process, "the coach really helped me to articulate my value proposition, helped me with reviewing my resume, identifying accomplishments. And then, in the interview process, [she] helped me to look at the challenges the position was offering and how that would help me fulfill my ultimate career goals." Within the next few months, she secured a new position at a higher level as associate general counsel in another hospital system.

Lisa was let go from her COO position shortly after we met, and it was very traumatic. She knew she had to quickly shift gears to find another position, but that's sometimes easier said than done. "That's the first time in my career I've been fired. I still sometimes have this sick little nausea in my stomach about it, but it passes. You were able to turn my attitude around so well that, when I went into those interviews, I was confident and interviewed extremely well."

Whether or not your career transition is due to your own initiative or a change imposed on you, it can be a scary time. Fear of change and lack of confidence can sabotage your efforts to land a new job. As your coach, I provide encouragement and support along with direction and feedback to get you through the transition and come out on top.

Jody has been looking for a new position for over a year when she took my workshop, "GPS Your Career." She was anxious to figure out how she could improve her résumé and interviewing skills. We began the process with identifying her value proposition, which translated into a more powerful résumé. We also discussed if the jobs she was applying for were a good fit. I then worked with her to better communicate her value proposition and potential to prospective employers. It helped her regain her lost confidence. We have only had a couple of sessions to date, but she is already much better positioned to get the job she wants.

Making a change is scary, and women are more resistant to change and taking risks than men. It is therefore more common for us to get complacent in a job that no longer challenges us. We love the people. The commute is good. Maybe it even suits our need to spend more time with our family. There are always valid reasons to stay put. At the end of the day, it depends on how important your ambition is. The point is, when you realize it's time to move on and seek more challenges and responsibility, that's a great time to work with a coach. Career transition is difficult regardless of the reason for the change.

Moving You Out of Your Comfort Zone to Reach Your Full Potential

It's a fact of human nature that we seek situations that make us feel comfortable. It's pretty frightening to change our behavior and let go of habits, even if we know that these behaviors and habits are holding us back from success. Intellectually, we may recognize the need to modify our approach, but it's not easy to do. One of the best benefits of working with a coach is that the coach helps you stretch and move out of your comfort zone so you can realize your ambitions.

I've witnessed many occasions in which women declare their ambition but never take action on it. This makes me sad because not only will they regret their lost opportunities at some point, but their company also loses the benefit of their talent and expertise. Often these women do not know how to move forward; they are fearful and don't understand how to make the necessary changes. This is where coaching makes a huge difference.

Take a good look at where you are now. How would a little bit of stretching improve your performance, reputation, and network? We all have room to stretch, and sometimes an extra effort and a commitment to move outside our comfort zone makes the difference between staying where we are and getting a promotion.

Sometimes that requires challenging yourself to promote yourself more and let others know your accomplishments. It may involve reaching out to new people to build relationships. It could also be speaking up and asking for what you want and need, including a mentor or sponsor. Maybe it's confronting your deepest fears about failure and success. If you are serious about your career, you will need to move outside your comfort zone. A coach's support and encouragement helps you leave the safety of your comfort zone to reach your potential.

Lisa summed up the benefits of coaching really well. She said she has read Marshall Goldsmith's *What Got You Here Won't Get You There*, and she believes that this is true about coaching for career advancement. You've gotten where you are now because of your hard work and talent, but that won't necessarily get you where you want to go. Working with a coach not only gives you strategy and direction but also provides the tools to move you forward with confidence.

What to Look for in a Coach

Probably the most important thing to consider when choosing a coach is chemistry. Regardless of the coach's background and experience, the only way the relationship will work for you is if your styles are compatible. Chemistry is best determined through personal interaction, either face-to-face or by phone or Skype. After all, it is a partnership and both parties need to have confidence in and respect for each other. A strong personal connection with your coach is critical.

Style is important, and everyone has their own preferences. Katherine was looking for a coach with the same work ethic and values. Lisa wanted someone who would give her honest feedback and straight answers without sugarcoating. Your coach's style should match your needs. I've had coaches who were very direct, and I've had coaches who were warm and fuzzy. You decide what you need for a good working relationship.

There are some common qualities to look for, however. A good coach is an excellent listener and is nonjudgmental. He or she actively listens and offers objective feedback and advice.

Your coach doesn't necessarily need to have experience in your industry, but I would highly recommend that the coach have a sound business and management background. Figuring out what type of support you need will lead you to the right coach. Diane is COO of a business, so she sought out a coach with broad business and management experience. Mona looked for someone who understood the people dynamics in the workplace because that was her focus and challenge.

Here are some questions to ask your prospective coach:

1. Where did you get your coach training?
2. Are you certified by the International Coach Federation?
3. How long have you been coaching?
4. Who is your typical client?
5. What is your business background?
6. How would you describe your coaching style?
7. Are your programs customized?
8. What are your different programs and fees?
9. How often do you meet with clients?
10. Do you meet live or by phone or Skype?
11. Do you use assessments? If so, which ones do you use?
12. Are you available to shadow me at work?
13. Do you coach both men and women?
14. What type of payment terms do you offer?
15. Can you share some relevant experiences you've had with clients?
16. Will you provide at least two references?

Additional things to note:

- Do they genuinely seem to be interested in you and your career?
- Are they pushing you to make a big financial commitment right away?
- Do you feel comfortable talking to them? Enough to share your innermost fears and doubts?
- Do they seem to understand your challenges and have some experience dealing with them?

Find the Right Coach

Coaching has gained tremendous popularity in the last decade, and therefore it is fairly easy to find a coach. Finding the right coach for you, however, needs to be an intentional and personal process.

Word of mouth is one of the best ways to get referrals for coaches. Ask trusted colleagues from inside or outside your company for referrals. Many of my clients come to me through other clients, especially when they witness the success of those clients over time. For example, Katherine's spectacular success led to me getting three more clients in that organization.

Tap into your network for recommendations. Lisa found me through a former colleague of hers. "I clearly trusted the person who told me about you. She said you've changed a lot of things for her. And I said to myself, 'How could this be? This sounds too good to be true.' But I trusted her judgment and then made that call."

Becky found her coach through some executive women at her company. "I sent a note out to them and said that I was looking for someone, and they recommended a firm."

When Mona was given a new position with more responsibility, she spoke with a colleague about coaching. "She explained what a coach could offer. I had not really understood this and thought it might be more 'mushy' than what she explained. I did research the coach before going to see her and explored what she had published and some of her videos. I also went to the first visit with her, assuming it was a test run." Mona went into the first session with an open mind and ended up hiring that coach.

Many of my clients find me by attending workshops or seminars where I present. This is another good way to meet and evaluate a prospective coach. After all, you get a good idea of the person's style, expertise, and message, and you can then determine if that person is a good fit for you.

Check with your alumni association for referrals. I am listed in the Harvard Business School directory for executive coaches; this list includes coaches, along with a description of their specialty. Your alumni association may also have this type of resource. Check their website or place a call to your alumni office and see if they have recommendations.

The International Coach Federation has a free online referral service that you can also check out.[6]

Once you've done the preliminary research, you will have a list of potential coaches. Reach out to them and set up time to talk on the phone or meet for coffee to narrow down your search. It's best to meet with a couple of coaches to determine if the chemistry is right and who will best support you and your specific needs. As we have discussed, many coaches offer complimentary coaching sessions. Take advantage of this offer because this one-on-one interaction gives you a lot of information about the coach's style and approach.

Individualized executive coaching may also be available through your organization. Many companies contract with coaching firms to support their executives and emerging leaders. If approved, the company may pay for the coaching or reimburse you. The best way to find this out is to ask HR. It would be helpful in this case to have the support of your boss and specific goals in mind to build your case for why you want and/or need coaching. Coaching may be positioned as part of your development plan.

Organizations also contract with outside firms to specifically coach their high-potential employees, and both group and individualized programs are offered in the workplace or at external venues. In this case, you need to be identified by your boss or Human Resources as a high-potential employee. Find out from HR if there is such a program and what the requirements are, as we discussed in Chapter 3.

If your company has agreed to provide coaching services for you, ask to interview a couple of approved coaches so that you can evaluate the best fit for you. If your company doesn't approve the services, you can still ask them to recommend coaches with whom they have had a positive experience.

Do your due diligence. Google your prospective coaches. Read their website and any articles they've written. Check out the books they've published as well. Connect with them on LinkedIn, Facebook, and Twitter and follow them. See if their messages and posts resonate with you.

Frame the Relationship

To maximize your work with a coach, it's important to establish realistic goals and time frames from the onset. Most coaches begin the relationship with a strategy session to better understand your expectations and objectives. Come prepared to that initial discussion with what you are trying to achieve, along with your challenges.

I recommend not only defining career goals but also establishing specific, measurable goals for the coaching as well. These goals should be reviewed periodically to evaluate the effectiveness of the coaching support and your commitment to do the work. Coaches will not necessarily offer any guarantees for reaching specific milestones because the partnership requires that both parties participate. Yet it is still a good idea to have some way to evaluate your progress.

It is quite possible that your goals and time frames will need to be modified over time. Revisit the plan on a regular basis to determine its ongoing validity. As previously noted, navigating the workplace presents unexpected situations, and a "recalculation" of direction may be necessary. There may be a reorganization that affects your role. You may have a new boss. A new opportunity may become available in a different business unit. The one thing you can count on is that change is inevitable, and many of these changes will require a new approach for you or an adjustment in your plan. A good coach will work with you to figure out the best way to move you forward, given any changes or hiccups that may occur.

Return on Investment

With a solid plan in place and realistic objectives and time frames, you can easily determine if your coaching relationship is successful. It may not always be quantifiable, however, as some goals are not financially driven.

I will say this, however: Coaching pays off if you are working with a good coach and you do the work! That being said, many of us are hesitant to invest in themselves and their careers. We struggle with the notion of putting ourselves on the forefront and following through with what we declare to be our career aspirations. We find every excuse not to spend the money on ourselves and make everything else a priority. So at the end of the day, you can do all the research and due diligence to find the right coach for you, but you need to take that leap of faith that you are worthy of the investment.

Our default behavior often is to take the back seat and put everyone else's wants and needs ahead of our own. Of course, this is fueled sometimes by our belief that we will be successful if we just keep our head down and work hard. If we just keep at it, we will eventually be successful. Well, we know that belief is not supported by current research.

What could possibly hold you back from making a commitment to coaching? It is possible that what you say you want isn't what you really want, and when it comes down to taking a big step toward your objective, you realize that it's not as important to you as you thought? But are you kidding yourself? Is it possible you're afraid of failure—or of success?

As you get closer to making a commitment and these feelings surface, you should to ask yourself what emotions are present. What would it take for you to feel comfortable with the decision to hire a coach? At the end of the day, it's usually a question of how much your career advancement means to you. It's scary to invest in yourself when you are not accustomed to doing so. But trust in yourself and your abilities. Believe that you deserve to move up!

All the women interviewed for this book proclaim coaching has been instrumental for them to get ahead and stay ahead. Many of my clients—Mary, Lisa, Katherine—were promoted at least once within the first year. They wanted it, and they were willing to do the necessary work to achieve their goals.

When I asked Lisa about the return on investment for her coaching, she said of her experience, "In the financial industry at the beginning of 2013, this 49-year-old woman goes and interviews for two big bank jobs and gets offers from both. Plus, I had two consulting gigs that people were offering me, too. So within eight weeks, I had two job offers. So, if you can't quantify that return on investment for coaching, I don't know."

Summary

Getting ahead and staying ahead in today's workplace is not easily accomplished. High-achieving women face many challenges in competitive male-dominated environments. Gender bias and office politics can derail them at any time. Internal barriers such as lack of confidence, hesitancy to self-promote and network, and avoidance of politics are also powerful factors that contribute to their lack of advancement.

The GPS helps you navigate the complexities of the workplace, overcome your limiting beliefs, and position yourself for success. It increases the effectiveness of the other tools in the Political Toolkit so that you reach your goals faster.

In This Chapter, We've Learned

- The definition of coaching.
- Why coaching is important for high-achieving women.
- How coaching works with the other tools in the Political Toolkit.

- The benefits of coaching and return on investment.
- The different types of coaching available.
- What to look for in a coach.
- How to find a coach.
- How to frame the coaching relationship to maximize effectiveness.

7

Staying Ahead

In this book so far we've discussed using the tools in the Political Toolkit to help you advance your career. Self-promotion, attention to workplace dynamics, strategic networking, sponsorship, and executive coaching all contribute to getting ahead as a woman in a competitive, often male-dominated work environment.

Now what happens when you get promoted? When you reach a leadership position? Can you put your tools away? NO! All the tools become even more important now to maintain your new status and title, and to protect your responsibilities and territory.

If you think it's hard to get promoted, you should be aware of the fact that it can be even more challenging to stay on top. It's certainly not a good time to put your head in the sand and retreat to your old habits of just focusing on the work and your performance. Unfortunately, that's what many women do.

Authors Herminia Ibarra, Robin Ely, and Deborah Kolb refer to the tendency of senior women to get bogged down in details and lose sight of the bigger picture. "In the upper echelons of organizations, women become increasingly scarce, which heightens the visibility and scrutiny of those near the top, who may become risk averse and overly focused on details and lose their sense of purpose."[1]

Your new position is not sacred, despite the fact that you are talented and deserving of the promotion. Complacency might have been tolerable once upon a time, but things change too fast in today's complex work environment, and many of these changes are not within your control. Therefore, it is critical that you stay relevant and that you're at the top of your game. As Kathleen Kelly Reardon writes in *The Secret Handshake*, "The prized executive offices are scarce, so competition is fierce. Yet at the loftier levels a high degree of professionalism is required. It's important for everyone to appear as though they are above pettiness and petulance. Consequently, political warfare at this level is subliminal and more often comprised of hidden minefields and stealth bombers than hand-to-hand combat. As the stakes get higher, the battle gets rougher, even if you can't see the weapons."[2]

Keeping an eye out for the ever-changing rules of the game is essential. Because the politics are more intense as you move up in the organization, your political skill becomes much more important than your technical skills. Political savvy is the key to both getting ahead and staying ahead. Your consistent and sophisticated approach to managing workplace politics is critical in order to survive and thrive in your new role.

At the senior level, political savvy is required to support your leadership position and takes on different necessities once you are promoted.

Political savvy helps with:

1. The need to manage your reputation and establish your authority as a leader.

   Your authority and expertise will be challenged in your new role, especially because you're a woman. Thus, there is an ongoing need to self-advocate and maintain your authority. All eyes are on the leadership in the organization, and political savvy helps you understand the optimal way to position yourself given the culture.

As Gerald R. Ferris, Sherry L. Davidson, and Pamela L. Perrewé write in *Political Skill at Work,* "Managers and executives must consciously manage the image they project, and do so to perfection, with political skill. The social astuteness and interpersonal influence facets of political skill play key roles here, and, of course, none of this works if not done convincingly, that is, in an apparently sincere and genuine way."[3]

2. The need to stay tuned in to the ever-changing dynamics of the work environment.

We know that change is inevitable and that even in the most stable organizations, change is a constant factor. Restructuring, mergers, and acquisitions bring about change. People leave their positions for a variety of reasons, and new people arrive. These unfamiliar managers and leaders come with their own agendas that need to be understood. And power plays occur on a regular basis, which require you to be sensitive to what's going on and who the key stakeholders are. This requires political savvy.

3. The need to have trusted relationships as resources and sources of information.

To be an effective manager and leader, you need a network of people you can rely on to get things done who will also advocate for your projects and initiatives. Building a network of people inside the organization who not only will help you accomplish your goals but also will provide information about the workplace dynamics is critical.

As a senior executive, you can easily be isolated from the reality of the workplace. Successful leaders consult with their trusted advisors for information and feedback. They establish a personal board of advisors inside and outside the organization to stay up to date on current business and industry practices. All these activities are fueled by political savvy.

4. The need to effectively communicate your vision and persuade and influence others to act.

As a leader, you achieve results through others, and the most effective leaders know how to inspire people to take action. To do this well, you must have the ability to read and understand people's motivations and interests. Successful leaders know how to line up support for their initiatives and create the right environment for change and innovation. It takes political skill to accomplish this.

The Danger of Being an Outsider

Regardless of your new title and position, being an outsider in your own organization is dangerous. You're an outsider when you fail to acknowledge and engage in the politics and when you neglect to use political savvy to build crucial relationships of trust and influence. As a result, you are isolated and especially vulnerable to any power plays. You lose your effectiveness as a leader because you lack a network of allies and champions who advocate for you and help you implement your initiatives. In essence, a leader who is an outsider is a lame duck.

The Center for Creative Leadership (CCL) studied why promising executives failed at the job and found that their "executive derailment" was primarily caused by a lack of social effectiveness.[4] Social effectiveness is political savvy. Without it, no matter how talented you are, you will not be successful as a leader.

Political savvy takes time to develop. Using all the tools in the Political Toolkit takes a dedicated focus. We can see just how important these tools are if we look at what happens when our ability to activate them is hampered due to circumstances.

Let's revisit the example of Sallie Krawcheck that we discussed in Chapter 1. Formerly with Merrill Lynch, Sallie was brought into Bank of America after it acquired Merrill in 2008. Once labeled the most powerful woman on Wall Street, she lost her senior position at Bank of America because she was an outsider to the bank's culture. As a result, she found it extremely challenging to negotiate the complex workplace dynamics. "Unhappily, my implicit bet that the parent company culture was one I could navigate effectively was incorrect. . . . But in fact, at this new shop, there was a melding of several cultures brought together through acquisition and changing through a leadership transition; thus, while I was learning the culture, it was itself shifting and changing."[5]

Sallie didn't have the advantage of knowing the rules of the game when she took this new position. She found it difficult to build strong relationships with key stakeholders and influencers to help her do her job well, and that cost her the job.

A recent study by Michelle K. Ryan and S. Alexander Haslam addresses the risky position women like Sallie Krawcheck are in when they are brought into an organization from the outside to manage the business through a crisis. Unable to build the social and political capital quickly enough, they are set up to fail. Ryan and Haslam referred to this as the "glass cliff."[6]

The immediate focus for these women executives is to get results. Their attention is not on the office politics per se. In other words, they don't have the luxury of time to build their political and social capital. As outsiders, it is extremely difficult for them to learn the unwritten rules and build strong relationships with the power brokers and influencers quickly enough to make their mark and be successful. It's as if their political skill is disabled, and they are trying to achieve results that usually are best accomplished through social and political power. They are teetering on the glass cliff without the awareness of their precarious position until it's too late.

Strategy&, the consulting firm formerly known as Booz & Company, released a study in May 2014 showing that "women are more often forced out of CEO jobs than men who hold the same position." In fact, in the decade preceding the report, "38 percent of female chief executives were asked to leave their positions (rather than leaving due to a retirement or merger), compared with 27 percent of male CEOs."[7] They concluded that the failure of this high percentage of women CEOs was due to the fact that they were brought into the organization from the outside. Their outsider status proved to be more challenging than the expectations of the CEO position. According to Gary Neilson, one of the Strategy& study's coauthors, "Being CEO as an outsider is a tougher job. They don't have as many connections in the company to understand how things work, and their performance is not as high" as employees who have developed over time. According to research cited in *The Washington Post,* "External CEOs are 6.7 times more likely to be dismissed with a short tenure than homegrown ones."[8]

I see the "glass cliff" example as a great reminder for all of us at all levels in an organization. Women like Sallie Krawcheck and Carol Bartz, the first female chief executive of Yahoo! who was hired in 2009 and fired in 2010, are extremely powerful and talented. That's why they were hired to manage a company in transition. But as the term "glass cliff" implies, they were set up to fail because they didn't have the opportunity as outsiders to learn the unwritten rules and build the relationships they needed to be successful.

This is an important lesson for you as you move up the ranks in an organization, because you can be an outsider even in your own company if you disconnect from the politics. If you don't use your Political Toolbox to manage your reputation, develop strong relationships, and pay attention to the workplace dynamics, you, too, may become an outsider—and then you create your own glass cliff!

How to Use the Political Toolkit to Stay Ahead

A committed and dedicated use of the Political Toolkit helped you get promoted. Each of the tools is important for your ongoing success, but now that you've been promoted to a more senior position, you will use them with a new focus. Let's explore how using these tools will help you be effective in your new position and support your status and continued advancement.

The Mirror

We previously used the Mirror to help you identify your unique value proposition. Understanding your value allowed you to authentically and confidently talk about your accomplishments and to gain access to the informal networks of influence in the organization.

Now the focus of your self-reflection has a slightly different purpose. With self-reflection you see your true self: your strengths, your vulnerabilities. This self-knowledge is necessary for effective leadership, because it helps you to identify your authentic style and lead from your personal power.

Women who don't take the time to use the Mirror to reflect and discover their personal power are often challenged to be authentic and effective leaders. Barbara Annis & Associates interviewed senior women leaders and asked them what were their greatest barriers. "Most all the women in our study acknowledge the challenges of working in male-dominated organization and, at times, struggling to exercise their own authentic style of leadership and management."[9]

The Mirror is especially effective for those women who want to lead and manage others and remain true to their values and core beliefs. Self-knowledge not only helps you remain authentic but also serves as your moral compass, which is especially helpful in times of crisis.

Charlotte Beers, former chairman of J. Walter Thompson and undersecretary for public diplomacy and public affairs for Secretary of State Colin Powell, says in her book, *I'd Rather Be in Charge*, "We are women. We will be tested. And in those tests, you need to know what you have inside that you can call on. Deeply felt self-knowledge is the key to unlocking your best and strongest self at work. This is what underlies the emotional intelligence that lets you empathize with and motivate others. It's also the source of the vaunted charisma we all wish to project as women in charge."[10]

The Mirror helps you to identify your strengths and weaknesses, giving you the opportunity to leverage those strengths to achieve results. This knowledge about yourself equips you to hire a strong, diverse team that compliments you. It gives you confidence to state your opinion and speak up with authority, and thereby helps you establish your reputation as a strong and decisive leader.

Self-knowledge gives you the confidence to listen and learn from others, and to be open to their ideas without feeling defensive or challenged.

We discussed how jumping in and doing the grunt work will prevent you from being seen as a leader. This still holds true at the senior level. You want to make sure that you are identifying and taking advantage of opportunities to showcase your leadership skills and not falling victim to your willingness and perhaps your comfort zone of doing all the work. Self-knowledge allows you to understand the best way you can add value to the organization without succumbing to taking on all the work and damaging your reputation as a leader.

Barbara Annis & Associates gives an example of this in *Solutions to Women's Advancement*. "A woman CFO is asked to present to the board and jumps in enthusiastically to do the background work. She spends the next two weeks laboring over the creation of a perfect and meaningful presentation to the board that would finally give her a seat at the table—and defeated her own purpose in doing so. She failed to distinguish between a management project and a leadership project, and it ended with her managing the work and the CEO seizing the leadership role."[11] In this case, the Mirror would have helped the CFO think strategically about how she could add value to best support this project and position herself as a leader rather than a doer.

Of course, after a promotion, you can't rest on your laurels when it comes to self-promotion either. There is an ongoing need at every level to advocate for yourself to manage your reputation and image. Ask your trusted advisors for feedback on a regular basis to make sure you are perceived as an effective leader and manager. Be open to making some changes if necessary. Use your value proposition to help the organization push initiatives forward.

We've discussed the importance of viewing self-promotion as a leadership skill. Once you have been promoted to a new position, continue to let key stakeholders know about what you and your team have accomplished. To establish yourself as a leader, take the time to think about the best way to leverage these results across the company for the overall benefit of the business. Continue to look for ways to build visibility and credibility.

It takes a village to build a successful career and business. In a leadership role, you need to motivate and inspire others to act. But the process begins with YOU first. As a leader, it's critical to take the time to reflect in order to create a powerful vision for the company. The Mirror can be extremely useful here as well.

Managing and growing a business involves risk taking. When you have confidence in your value proposition, it is easier to evaluate business opportunities. As we have discussed, recognizing where you can add value to the business positions you to take some risky but highly visible assignments, and to make some bold decisions about where to take the business—all of which differentiates you in a crowded space and contributes to your success as a leader.

The Magnifying Glass

The Magnifying Glass helped you figure out the workplace dynamics and understand how decisions are made in your organization. It helped you identify those with power and influence. All this knowledge allowed you to navigate the realities of your organization and position yourself for a promotion.

Once you are promoted, continuing to use the Magnifying Glass is critical for your ongoing success. It fulfills the ongoing need to stay tuned in to any fluctuations in the workplace. Your focused attention to this protects you from potential power plays that can rob you of your power or position. The information you gather from your consistent observation assists you in identifying possible roadblocks.

Your Magnifying Glass gives you a reality check. What's happening in the organization? What's changed? What needs to change? Observing the workplace dynamics gives you the political savvy to position yourself well, establish your leadership, and adjust to any fluctuations if necessary.

As Kathleen Kelly Reardon writes in *It's All Politics,* "Whether at the very top of organizations or farther down the ladder, the politically astute stay in touch with what is going on around them and communicate with others in ways that align their goals with those in power or soon to be in power. They make it their business to know a great deal about the systems in which they work, the common views that define those systems as well as loopholes in those common views, and the kind of behavior considered controversial. They know how to talk so that others are compelled to listen. Well in advance of any serious conflict, they develop an arsenal of options and a corral of connections that can help make those options possible."[12]

Two of my coaching clients, Mary and Joanne, recently moved to more senior positions in new organizations this year. Our immediate focus was to understand the political landscape, identify who has power and influence, and observe how decisions are made. This initial attention and sensitivity to the politics helped both Mary and Joanne transition quickly from outsider to insider status and gave them the necessary information to build key relationships that best support their success. These relationships now include senior management as well as colleagues, direct reports, and lower and midlevel managers. The Magnifying Glass is an essential tool to monitor the complete political landscape.

In Chapter 4, we examined the subtleties of gender bias in today's workplace. As you move up the ladder as a woman and assume more responsibility, you will be exposed to more gender-related attitudes people may associate with leadership and assertive communication. Your attention to these attitudes and the people who manifest them will help you assess the landscape, navigate successfully, and align yourself with allies. It assists you in identifying potential saboteurs who can undermine your authority.

Not only does the Magnifying Glass protect your status against future power plays and help you find champions and allies, but it also enables you to see the details of the politics, conflict, and issues that need to be resolved. As a leader you can use the information to resolve problems with a keen eye on the bigger picture. This intelligence is invaluable for your ongoing success, and it is there right under your nose if you take the time to see it.

As with the Mirror and the other tools in the Political Toolkit, your commitment of time and focus to use these tools will determine your ongoing success. Says Reardon in *It's All Politics*, "Political acumen is largely learned from observation. And then it's a matter of practice, practice, practice, and more practice."[13]

The Pass Go and Collect $200 Card

The Pass Go Card was especially effective in helping you build a network of people who supported your advancement and perhaps opened the door for new opportunities for you. Now you must continue to nurture the relationships you have with your current contacts while strategically seeking people who will support you in your present position. These additional contacts will not only provide information and resources for you to get the job done but also should include champions to advocate for your leadership initiatives.

Ferris and his coauthors cite research stating that "effective managers spend nearly half their time on networking activities, much more than they devote to what would be considered traditional managerial activities. Leadership involves goal accomplishment with and through others and the social capital that accrues to those with political skill is what makes it possible for leaders to be effective, thus further illustrating the critical role such skill plays in organizational life."[14]

While using the Mirror helps you identify your value proposition, the Pass Go Card provides you with a platform to communicate your value and enhance your reputation. This leads to a solid framework of connections that give you informal and formal advice, and also provide you with important information about the work environment.

In your new leadership role, you may also turn to your network outside your current company when you're hiring and putting together your new team. Who do you trust? Who have you worked with? You may want to establish your own team of people that have proven their loyalty and delivered results.

When I was hired as a president and CEO for one of the Service-Master companies, I inherited a senior management team that had worked with the previous CEO. I knew it would take time to evaluate their effectiveness, and my immediate goal was to grow the business through hospital joint ventures. So I turned to my network and hired a former colleague as my SVP of Sales. I knew he had strong relationships with hospital management and a great track record of closing deals. I trusted him and wanted him on my team. Phillip hit the ground running and quickly blended in with the COO and CFO. Later he became a great source of informal information for me, letting me know about the internal politics at play.

The Pass Go Card also helps you look for new opportunities to advance your career. Chris Reilly, who we met in Chapter 4, says that networking is critical for this purpose at the senior level. "There are circumstances that you can't control, like a chairman and CEO moves on, gets booted, whatever the reasons are, and that has profound implications for you. When this happened at CIT, I was pretty practical that it was just a matter of time before somebody showed up at my office door looking for my head. So I decided this was the right time for me to take control of my life and be proactive. I knew I had some time and it wasn't going to happen right away, but that's when relationships become really, really important, and you can go to friends and colleagues at a senior level and a lot of information gets shared. Most of the important information is informal; it's all under the table. And being plugged into that is really important in terms of being able to figure out which way the political winds are shifting."

"A lot of senior level positions are not broadcast; they're all under the cover when you get to that upper echelon. And stuff's going on in the background, and it's not like you're going to go on company ABC's job postings and see it listed there. The executive and senior positions never get filled that way. So you really need to be plugged in."

Your networking must continue throughout your career, and the people in your network will change based on your position, your company, and your career goal. As your work experience grows, your network should expand to include current and former colleagues. These relationships will prove invaluable for your continued success. Over the course of your career, your network becomes your net worth.

The Get Out of Jail Free Card

Sponsors are important to get ahead as well as to maintain your status. The Get Out of Jail Free Card assists you in selecting the right type of sponsor support as you move up the hierarchy. And as we mentioned in Chapter 5, you should develop relationships with more than one sponsor from inside as well as outside your organization.

One sponsor may help you get promoted, as we learned with Katherine in Chapter 5. But other sponsors can give you global visibility to help you increase your executive reach and expand your influence. In other words, don't put all your eggs in one sponsor's basket. Continue to seek out the support this type of relationship can provide even after you have been promoted. Keep your focus on where you want to go in the long term, and seek sponsors who can help you be effective in your current role as well as help you move to the next level.

Having sponsors outside the organization contributes to your increased visibility and will support you during a pending career move that may become necessary due to circumstances or personal choice. After all, most company reorganizations result in a new leadership team, and those executives frequently want to bring in their own team of talent. You can call upon sponsors to open up doors for new opportunities; your Magnifying Glass and Pass Go Card also will help you to be proactive in this regard.

If you are now in a leadership role, you should consider sponsoring another talented high-potential woman in your organization. Very often sponsors intentionally seek protégés to help them expand their network and workplace intelligence. The protégés may also have certain experiences and talents that will strengthen your position as a leader, as we discussed in Chapter 5.

The GPS

The GPS, your executive coach, helped you get promoted by providing a strategic plan for you to navigate the workplace, holding you accountable to implement that plan, and offering guidance to overcome your internal barriers to success. Working with a coach accelerated your advancement. The political skills you learned with your coach are especially helpful now that you have been promoted. As you gain more responsibility and status and as the competition escalates, you must call upon these skills more than ever. In fact, it is your political skill, not your technical skills, that will ensure your success at a senior level.

As we discussed earlier in this chapter, the CCL studied why promising executives fail to be successful, and they found the major cause to be a lack of political and social skills. Their study concluded that "political savvy and interpersonal issues appear to be far more difficult than technical issues for many people to master on their own. When they find themselves in positions that require political skill, those fortunate enough to recognize the problems are increasingly calling on executive coaches for assistance."[15] In fact, CCL recommends working with an executive coach for at least one year.

This recommendation is based on their belief that "a skilled coach can help you become more conscious of politically charged environments and more astute at observing political situations and people. Over time and with practice, you can refine novice skills into a well-integrated skill inventory and smooth style that will help you deal effectively with a wide array of situations."[16]

Another important reason to work with a coach is to help you transition to your new role. This is one challenge that is often overlooked when moving into a leadership position.

In their 2013 *Harvard Business Review* article, Ibarra and her coauthors wrote about the challenge of this transition: "Learning how to be an effective leader is like learning any complex skill: It rarely comes naturally and usually takes a lot of practice. Successful transitions into senior management roles involve shedding previously effective professional identities and developing new, more fitting ones. Yet people often feel ambivalent about leaving the comfort of roles in which they have excelled, because doing so means moving toward an uncertain outcome."[17]

Michelle Keefe, COO of Touchpoint Solutions, turned to an executive coach during her transition to her new leadership role. "When I transitioned out of pharma and into the health care not-for-profit sector, I engaged the support of an executive coach. Although you know many of the right things to do in a transition, an executive coach helps you think through the very specific approach you will take to inspire and lead a new team, learning the culture, identifying quick wins you can have in the business, and helps you with prioritizing the change and goals. In essence, an executive coach helps to ensure you do not try to boil the ocean! I had great success in this new role due to proper planning and a laser focus on how I approached each situation and how I built relationships with key stakeholders and team members. This is an investment I made myself and has contributed greatly to my success."

Your continued work with a coach also gives you insight into what specific leadership and management skills need to be strengthened for you to be successful in your role and position you for future advancement. As we discussed in Chapter 6, this becomes the basis for your ongoing action plan with your coach. A skilled coach identifies resources for you to boost your skill set and gives you exercises to expand specific leadership and management skills.

Coaching Helps You Cope with the Pressure of Your New Position

The stress on today's leaders, especially women leaders, can be overwhelming. We face greater scrutiny in the upper tiers of the organization, in part due to the heightened visibility but also due to the scarcity of women in these leadership roles. This scrutiny becomes more intense the higher up we go.

The negative voices in your head, often referred to as "gremlins," get louder with increased pressure from work, and they sabotage your best efforts to succeed. Your deepest fears begin to surface as you question your competence and your ability to succeed in a leadership role that brings expanded visibility. You worked hard to get promoted, but once you achieve your goal, you wonder if you deserve it. You second-guess yourself, are afraid to take risks, and lose your personal power and effectiveness.

It's always surprising to me how many successful women lack confidence and believe it was pure luck for them to be promoted. Some focus on perfectionism. Some fear failure, and some fear success. These limiting beliefs and habits don't stop once you are promoted. In fact, they can become more powerful when you are feeling more stressed. Any one of these gremlins can sabotage you if left unattended.

Coping with the pressure of assuming a new leadership role and your ongoing battle with your gremlins are important reasons to work with a coach. An example of how these limiting beliefs can undermine you was accurately described in Chapter 6 with Lisa's notion that she was an imposter despite her appointment to a senior position. Limiting beliefs distort reality and often lead you to make bad decisions and judgments about people and situations.

If you are prone to listening to your negative self-talk when stressed, you will be more vulnerable to their negative influence as you move up to a senior position. Your coach can be especially helpful in identifying any fears that hold you back from being an effective leader and/or advancing your career further. As we discussed in Chapter 6, a skilled coach gives you the support and tools to cope with and overcome old beliefs and behaviors that may keep you from being effective in your new role. Once you understand how these gremlins prevent you from being effective and reaching your potential, you are ready to let them go and find healthier beliefs that support your success. It's not easy, but the ongoing support and feedback from your coach and colleagues will keep you on track.

Coaching Helps You Overcome Your Superwoman Complex

Tara, a new client of mine, is a COO for retail banking and wealth management at a large global organization. She is ready, willing, and able to take on a new position in Europe that will be official in the next couple of weeks. Her promotion is well deserved. She is talented, and her track record is exceptional. She has worked hard for this promotion.

But one of Tara's major issues as a mother of two young children and a senior manager is managing her workload and her family obligations. Once promoted, she will need to maintain her current relationships in the United States while building new relationships in the London corporate office and learning a new role. This will put additional pressure and stress on her and her family.

This is an ongoing concern for young senior executive women whom I coach. Three of my clients have come up with a solution. Their husbands stay home with the children and take care of the household responsibilities. This solution obviously won't work for every family. But in most cases, when you reach the upper echelons of an organization, you can finally afford to relinquish some of your domestic responsibilities and hire childcare. But are you willing to do that? Do you still have a need to do it all?

Those of us who are mothers and career women have choices to make every step of the way. A skilled coach can help you make those choices, ditch some of the guilt, and understand the ongoing challenges of having a family and a successful career.

As a recovering superwoman myself, I am well acquainted with these challenges. I started my own career as a divorced mother of two young children. I traveled a great deal but still baked cookies for school parties and showed up at Little League games. I couldn't let go of any of my responsibilities as a mother, nor could I compromise my work. I was a stress case!

My children were grown by the time I reached the CEO level, but working my way up was difficult given everything I had on my plate. What I know from my own life experience is that our inability to let go of the superwoman complex can sabotage both our careers and our families. This is an ongoing dilemma for young, ambitious women, and a coach can help you stay on track.

Summary

The tools that helped you get promoted (the Mirror, the Magnifying Glass, the Pass Go Card, the Get Out of Jail Free Card, and the GPS) are the same tools that will help you to maintain your status and continue to advance your career. You will use these tools with a different focus to support where you are now in the organization, but the basic principles apply. All the tools work together to support your goals of getting ahead and staying ahead.

In This Chapter, We've Learned

- As you get promoted to more senior positions, the competition and scrutiny increase.

- Political skill becomes more important than technical skill in leadership roles.
- How political savvy helps us succeed in leadership roles.
- How to use the tools in the Political Toolkit to protect your job and position you for continued success.

8

Moving Forward

Are You Ready?

P olitical skills are essential career competencies to get ahead and stay ahead, and they are especially important for high-achieving women working in competitive male-dominated organizations.

We've taken a good look at the dynamics of the workplace: the politics at play, the subtle gender bias, the culture. We know that it's challenging for women to survive and thrive in these organizations. There are many obvious and hidden forces that can work against us as we move up the hierarchy. And we've seen how our own internal barriers keep us from engaging and reaching our full potential, our mind-set about politics being dirty and a waste of time, and our belief that focusing on the work alone will get us ahead, along with other negative beliefs about our competence.

We've also learned, however, that once we adopt a new mind-set about workplace politics and take the time to acquire new skills and practices through the use of the Political Toolkit, we can realize our goals. Using the tools—the Mirror, the Magnifying Glass, the Pass Go and Collect $200 Card, the Get Out of Jail Free Card, and the GPS—is a proven process that will help us get the promotion we deserve.

Now What?

You understand the issues and the obstacles. You have learned how the tools in the Political Toolkit help you to navigate the realities of the workplace. Are you ready to move forward?

Here's what I know from coaching professional women for almost a decade. Many women say they want to reach leadership positions. They proclaim their ambition and dedication, yet when push comes to shove, they back off. Of course, there are many reasons why women opt out or remain stuck in their current positions; timing is everything, and it has to be the right time for them to focus on their career path. But it's a choice: a choice to move forward or to stay put.

If you decide to make a commitment to your career with the goal of advancing to a leadership position, please know this is not for the faint of heart. It takes more than your talent and hard work to get there. It takes a dedicated focus and using all the tools in the Political Toolkit consistently. The process I've defined in this book is easy to follow, and with the proper support, you will learn to be savvy and gain the social and political capital required to get ahead.

Where Do You Go from Here?

The best place to begin your work toward getting a promotion is to figure out where you are now. What is your current mind-set about office politics? About using the tools? Are you ready to change some of your thinking and behavior to support your success?

Ask yourself these questions:

1. Am I willing to see office politics in a positive light as a means toward building relationships and influence?
2. Am I ready to let go of the idea that my work alone will get me promoted?
3. Am I willing to take the time to build social and political capital?

4. Am I willing to explore my own internal barriers to success?
5. Am I ready to commit to learn how to use the tools in the Political Toolkit to reach my career goal?

In Chapter 1, you took the Political Skills Assessment. You identified what skills you need to strengthen relative to self-promotion, strategic networking, and political savvy. Take the assessment again now to determine if there have been any changes since you started reading this book and began using some of the tools.

Use your current score to identify where you need to focus your attention and how best to prioritize your activities. What areas challenge you the most?

Where Do You Feel the Most Resistance?

Let's take a serious look at any resistance you might have to using the tools in the Political Toolkit, because this resistance is most likely caused by fear and must be addressed for you to move forward with enthusiasm.

Self-Promotion

When you think about promoting yourself in the workplace, what thoughts immediately pop into your head?

It is my experience that one of the most common fears women associate with self-promotion is the belief that self-promotion means bragging, and if you brag, people won't like you. Do you believe this?

The idea of promoting yourself by tooting your horn is not only uncomfortable for most women but also has the potential to backfire. We work in an environment that is not always welcoming to confident, assertive women. The optimal way for you to advocate for yourself, therefore, is not by memorizing a pitch and bragging. It just doesn't work. But at the same time, it does not serve you well to take a back seat and let others take credit for your accomplishments. Nor does it serve you to remain invisible. What does benefit you AND the organization is for you to understand the value you contribute and then offer to help others reach their business goals based on that value.

Remember, the Mirror helps you to identify your unique value proposition: how you contribute to successful business outcomes based on who you are and how you do the work. This is powerful information that will not only let others see you as a top contributor but also will help the organization leverage your talent and results to improve the business. You don't have to toot a loud horn for people to recognize your talent! Your offer to assist others with their initiatives based on your value proposition is a win-win experience. It helps you turn people on, not off. They will be excited to work with you and will recognize your contribution.

Put yourself in someone else's shoes for a minute. You have been working on a project and have encountered many obstacles. You can't seem to get the program on track, and it's about to implode, with serious consequences. Along comes a colleague who has a possible solution and is willing to help. You are grateful for the assistance and for the colleague's unique contribution to make the project successful, right? So, by lending your expertise to a project, you are not only helping the colleague but also gaining valuable exposure and credibility. Isn't this a terrific way to spread the word about your talent without bragging?

Making this shift in your thinking about self-promotion is critical for your success. Once you've made the shift, it's time to pick up the Mirror, identify your value proposition, and practice communicating this to colleagues and key stakeholders. For many women, this takes practice, practice, and more practice. For others, once they get their value proposition, they are off and running, because it's been the piece they've been missing for their whole career. Now they get it and can authentically and confidently talk about how they add value.

Figure 8.1 is your action plan for self-promotion. Identify and commit to taking three action steps in the next couple of weeks to create visibility for yourself in your organization.

Self-Promotion

Specific Measurable Action	By When?	Accountability / Support / Resources

FIGURE 8.1 Self-Promotion Action Plan

Observing the Workplace Dynamics

The only resistance I can imagine women having about using the Magnifying Glass is that they don't have the time. But that's a weak excuse. Quite honestly, none of my clients have resisted doing the work in this area. The work involved does not usually trigger any fears. It's a passive activity that follows their intention to understand the politics and culture in order to advance their career.

Review Chapter 3 and commit to taking three action steps to observe the politics and culture in the workplace, identify the decision makers and key stakeholders for your career, and set realistic time frames (see Figure 8.2).

Observing the Workplace

Specific Measurable Action	By When?	Accountability / Support / Resources

FIGURE 8.2 Observing the Workplace

Networking

What holds you back from networking? Many women tell me they don't have time to network. They are juggling two full-time jobs: work and family. And my advice to these women is to schedule at least one lunch or coffee per week for networking. You can accomplish building relationships during office hours without stressing out. Maybe once a month, you can go to some outside event after work, but choose wisely.

The issue of time can be solved quite easily, but when I'm coaching my clients, I often hear the more challenging issues and fears that prevent them from reaching out to other people. They don't know how to do it! They are afraid to extend themselves, and as a result, they spend their networking time within their comfort zone with people they already know and like. Unfortunately, that doesn't get them promoted.

I realize that Chapter 4, which is about the Pass Go Card, strategic networking, is ambitious. Adopting the mind-set about building a strategic network to support your professional growth is a new concept for most women. Trying to identify these people and meet with them can seem overwhelming. So let's break it down and take baby steps.

First, do the research suggested in Chapter 3 with your Magnifying Glass. Look at the people with whom you have the strongest relationships who might be connectors for you. Meet with a couple of them. Ask for their help and an introduction to someone you would like to meet. Perhaps they will accompany you for a coffee date with that person, but at the very least, ask them for a warm introduction, a door opener. Ask them if there is anything you can do for them in return.

Once you schedule a meeting with these new contacts, do some additional research about them. It would be helpful if the colleague who is introducing you has some information as well. Look them up on LinkedIn. Where did they go to school? Where do they live? How long have they worked for this company? Look for some commonality. And when you meet with them, ask them some

Networking

Specific Measurable Action	By When?	Accountability / Support / Resources

FIGURE 8.3 Networking

questions about themselves to start the conversation without being too personal. People love to talk about themselves, and it's a great way to start the conversation and a relationship.

The point here is that if the idea of developing a strategic network is daunting for you, start slowly, one person at a time. Yes, it is important to have this network of support, but if you get overwhelmed, you are more likely to back off and not do it at all.

Acknowledge what holds you back and practice making connections, not excuses. You can overcome the time constraints, but other fears may be sabotaging your efforts to build your support system.

Review your Power Network from Chapter 4 and use Figure 8.3 to identify three action steps to expand your current network in a realistic time frame.

Sponsorship

If you could have a sponsor, wouldn't you want one? Absolutely! But I find that even when women understand how powerful this relationship can be for them, they don't pursue it. They don't know how to approach potential sponsors and are afraid to ask. Well, of course it can be scary if you don't have a solid relationship with the person to begin with. This type of relationship doesn't develop overnight. Like any other relationship, it needs to be nurtured.

Sponsorship

Specific Measurable Action	By When?	Accountability / Support / Resources

FIGURE 8.4 Sponsorship

The first step is to identify potential sponsors. Then begin to sow the seeds for sponsorship. Choose projects that align with their interests and have visibility with them. Get on committees where they participate. Build a solid, trusting relationship over time.

Sometimes you don't even have to ask for a sponsor. These relationships may develop organically. But let your potential sponsor know what your career aspirations are and don't hesitate to talk about sponsorship when appropriate.

One step at a time still moves you forward in the direction of establishing this relationship. Make it your intention to work on building these relationships every week.

Review Chapter 5, which is about the the Get Out of Jail Free Card, and make a commitment to take three action steps to identify and build relationships with potential sponsors in the next 90 days (see Figure 8.4).

Executive Coaching

You may open up a Pandora's box of limiting beliefs when you consider hiring a coach: Am I worth the investment of hiring a coach? What happens if I commit to coaching and it doesn't work? What happens if it *does* work? Am I ready for success?

We talked about the return on investment for coaching at length in Chapter 6, so I won't belabor the point. I do know this: If you are

Coaching

Specific Measurable Action	By When?	Accountability / Support / Resources

FIGURE 8.5 Coaching

working with a skilled coach and you do the work, you will move your career forward. My clients have realized a return on investment with promotions and new job opportunities. They were serious about their ambition, and they did the work.

How committed are you to your career? Are you ready to take this step?

Review Chapter 6, the GPS, and use Figure 8.5 to identify three action steps to find and hire the right coach and commit to a realistic time frame.

Staying the Course

Sometimes the going gets tough. I don't want to sugarcoat the truth. It can take all our dedication and determination to stay the course and to continue to excel at what we do, while ducking and swerving from oncoming obstacles. Sometimes we just get tired of being the only chick in the room! Our quest to realize our ambition can drain our energy. We have to fight our desire to quit or to opt out.

Every day we have a choice to make. Are we on the right path? Is this the right company with the right culture to showcase my skills and talent? Is it worth it?

Of course, many women do opt out, especially when they've reached the stage of financial freedom. But the women who succeed are those who are committed to making a difference for themselves and the business. They have a passion and purpose to their careers. Successful women embrace the challenges of working in a male-dominated culture and set their intention on finding ways to increase their effectiveness as leaders.

I know that the journey to promotion is a lot easier when you are savvy as well as smart and you understand how to maximize your talent so that you have a positive impact on the business. Having the tools and knowing how to use them to improve your social effectiveness in the workplace will accelerate your advancement.

We already know you are talented and work hard. You've earned recognition and rewards for your contribution to the business. You deserve to move up. But we also know that a promotion will not fall in your lap just because you work hard. It takes a dedicated focus and continued intention to succeed. You now have the tools you need— the Mirror, the Magnifying Glass, the Pass Go Card, the Get Out of Jail Free Card, and the GPS—to develop your political savvy and get ahead. Use the tools and practice, practice, practice.

Do the work and you will succeed!

Notes

Chapter 1 Politics in the Workplace

1. Sallie Krawcheck, "What I Learned When I Got Ousted from Bank of America," *Quartz*, October 23, 2013, http://qz.com/138512 /sallie-krawcheck-what-i-learned-when-i-got-ousted-from-bank-of-america/.
2. Ibid.
3. http://maristpoll.marist.edu/wp-content/misc/nycpolls/c110322 /Bloomberg_Education/Complete%20April%204th,%202011%20NYC %20Poll%20Release%20and%20Tables.pdf.
4. www.catalyst.org/knowledge/women-ceos-fortune-1000.
5. Fred R. Blass, Robyn L. Brouer, Pamela L. Perrewé, and Gerald R. Ferris, "Politics Understanding and Networking Ability as a Function of Mentoring: The Roles of Gender and Race," *Journal of Leadership & Organizational Studies* 14, no. 2 (2007): 93–105, jlo.sagepub.com /content/14/2/93.
6. Pamela L. Perrewé and Debra L. Nelson, "Gender and Career Success: The Facilitative Role of Political Skill," *Organizational Dynamics* 33, no. 4 (2004): 371.
7. Kathleen Kelly Reardon, *It's All Politics: Winning in a World Where Hard Work and Talent Aren't Enough* (New York: Doubleday, 2005), 5.
8. Gerald R. Ferris and Darren C. Treadway, *Politics in Organizations: Theory and Research Considerations* (New York: Taylor & Francis, 2012), 532.
9. Perrewé and Nelson, "Gender and Career Success," 367.
10. Lisa Mainiero, "On Breaking the Glass Ceiling: The Political Seasoning of Powerful Women Executives," *Organizational Dynamics* 22, no. 4 (1994): 7.
11. Perrewé and Nelson, "Gender and Career Success," 366–67.

217

Chapter 2   The Mirror

1. Nancy M. Carter and Christine Silva, *The Myth of the Ideal Worker: Does Doing All the Right Things Really Get Women Ahead?* (New York: Catalyst, 2011), http://www.catalyst.org/publication/509/the-myth-of-the-ideal-worker-does-doing-all-the-right-things-really-get-women-ahead.
2. Marguerite Rigoglioso, "Researchers: How Women Can Succeed in the Workplace," *Insights* (blog), Stanford Graduate School of Business, March 1, 2011, http://www.gsb.stanford.edu/news/research/womencareer researchbyoreilly.html.
3. www.podcastdirectory.com for podcasts or look up Internet radio shows at www.blogtalkradio.com.

Chapter 3   The Magnifying Glass

1. Barbara Annis, Carolyn Lawrence, and Patsy Doerr, "Solutions to Women's Advancement," Barbara Annis & Associates in partnership with Thomson Reuters and Women of Influence, Canada, 2014, http://www .womenofinfluence.ca/wp-content/uploads/2014/04/Women-of-Influence-WhitePaper-2014.pdf, 13.
2. Ibid., 20.
3. Douglas A. Ready, Jay A. Conger, and Linda A. Hill, "Are You a High Potential?" *Harvard Business Review,* June 2010, http://hbr.org/2010/06 /are-you-a-high-potential/ar/1.
4. Emma Jacobs, "Sponsors Can Break Glass Ceiling for Female Employees," *The Globe and Mail,* July 29, 2013, http://www.theglobeandmail .com/report-on-business/careers/career-advice/sponsors-can-break-glass-ceiling-for-female-employees/article13484804.
5. Annis et al., *Solutions to Women's Advancement,* 20.
6. Erin Meyer, *The Culture Map: Breaking through the Invisible Boundaries of Global Business* (New York: Public Affairs, 2014), 25.
7. Alison Maitland, coauthor of *The Future World of Work*, interview by Bonnie Marcus, April 30, 2014.
8. Ibid.

Chapter 4 The Pass Go and Collect $200 Card

1. *Professional Networking and Its Impact on Career Advancement: A Study of Practices, Systems and Opinions of High-Earning, Elite Professionals* (Mountain View, CA: Upwardly Mobile, Inc., and Pepperdine Graziadio School of Business Management, 2008), http://www.belladomain.com /wp-content/uploads/2010/05/effective_networker_study.pdf.
2. Annis et al., *Solutions to Women's Advancement,* 19.
3. Ibid.
4. Ronald S. Burt, "Neighbor Networks: Understanding the Power of Networks," *Capital Ideas,* October 2009, http://www.chicagobooth.edu /capideas/oct09/2.aspx.
5. Sylvia Ann Hewlett, Kerrie Periano, Laura Sherbin, and Karen Sumberg, *The Sponsor Effect: Breaking through the Last Glass Ceiling* (Boston: Center for Work-Life Policy and Harvard Business Review, December 2010), http://hbr.org/product/the-sponsor-effect-breaking-through-the-last-glass/an/10428-PDF-ENG, 6.
6. *Professional Networking,* 5.
7. Ibid.
8. Ibid., 4.
9. Erin Meyer, interview by Bonnie Marcus, June 6, 2014.

Chapter 5 The Get Out of Jail Free Card

1. Sylvia Ann Hewlett, "The Real Benefit of Finding a Sponsor," *Harvard Business Review Blog Network,* January 26, 2011, http://blogs.hbr.org /2011/01/the-real-benefit-of-finding-a/.
2. Bob Moritz, chairman and senior partner, PricewaterhouseCoopers, interview with Bonnie Marcus, January 28, 2014.
3. Hewlett, "The Real Benefit."
4. Hewlett et al., *The Sponsor Effect,* 8.
5. Hewlett, "The Real Benefit."
6. Sylvia Ann Hewlett, "The Right Way to Find a Career Sponsor," *Harvard Business Review Blog Network,* September 11, 2013, http://blogs.hbr.org /2013/09/the-right-way-to-find-a-career-sponsor/.

7. Sylvia Ann Hewlett, "What Women Need to Advance: Sponsorship," *Forbeswoman* (blog), August 25, 2011, http://www.forbes.com/sites /sylviaannhewlett/2011/08/25/what-women-need-to-advance-sponsorship.

8. DiversityInc, "The 2014 DiversityInc Top 50 Companies for Diversity," accessed October 14, 2014, http://www.diversityinc.com/the-diversity inc-top-50-companies-for-diversity-2014.

9. Working Mother, "The 2014 NAFE Top 50 Companies for Executive Women," accessed October 14, 2014, http://www.workingmother.com /best-company-list/151009.

10. Hewlett, "The Right Way."

11. Sylvia Ann Hewlett, *Forget a Mentor, Find a Sponsor* (Boston: Harvard Business School Publishing, 2013), 90.

12. Hewlett, "The Right Way."

13. Sylvia Ann Hewlett, Melinda Marshall, and Laura Sherbin, "The Relationship You Need to Get Right," http://hbr.org/2011/10/the-relationship-you-need-to-get-right/ar/.

Chapter 6   The GPS

1. International Coach Federation, "Coaching FAQs," accessed October 14, 2014, http://www.coachfederation.org/need/landing.cfm?ItemNumber= 978&navItemNumber=567.

2. Alice H. Eagly and Linda L. Carli, *Through the Labyrinth: The Truth about How Women Become Leaders* (Boston: Harvard Business School Publishing, 2007), 1.

3. Perrewé and Nelson, "Gender and Career Success," 376.

4. Suzette Skinner, "Coaching Women in Leadership or Coaching Women Leaders? Understanding the Importance of Gender and Professional Identity Formation in Executive Coaching for Women" (white paper, May 2012), http://www.instituteofcoaching.org/images/Articles/Women inLeadershipResearchMay2012.pdf, 45.

5. Betsy Myers, *Take the Lead* (New York: Atria Books, 2011), 11–12.

6. International Coach Federation, "Coach Referral Service," accessed October 14, 2014, http://www.coachfederation.org/clients/crs/.

Chapter 7 Staying Ahead

1. Herminia Ibarra, Robin Ely, and Deborah Kolb, "Women in Leadership" *Harvard Business Review,* September 2013, 7.
2. Kathleen Kelly Reardon, *The Secret Handshake: Mastering the Politics of the Business Inner Circle* (New York: Doubleday, 2001), 2.
3. Gerald R. Ferris, Sherry L. Davidson, and Pamela L. Perrewé, *Political Skill at Work: Impact on Work Effectiveness* (Mountain View, CA: Davies-Black Publishing, 2005), 130.
4. Ibid., 38.
5. Krawcheck, "What I Learned."
6. Michelle K. Ryan and S. Alexander Haslam, "The Glass Cliff: Evidence That Women Are Overrepresented in Precarious Leadership Positions," *British Journal of Management* 16, no. 2 (2005): 81–90, http://papers.ssrn.com/sol3/papers.cfm?abstract_id=734677.
7. Jena McGregor, "Here's Why Women CEOs Are More Likely to Get Sacked from Their Jobs," May 2, 2014, http://www.washingtonpost.com/blogs/on-leadership/wp/2014/05/02/heres-why-women-ceos-are-more-likely-to-get-sacked-from-their-jobs/.
8. Ibid.
9. Annis et al., *Solutions to Women's Advancement,* 14.
10. Charlotte Beers, *I'd Rather Be in Charge: A Legendary Business Leader's Roadmap for Achieving Pride, Power, and Joy at Work* (New York: Vanguard Press, 2012), 102.
11. Annis et al., *Solutions to Women's Advancement,* 19.
12. Reardon, *It's All Politics,* 4.
13. Ibid., 8.
14. Ferris et al., *Political Skill at Work,* 130.
15. Ibid., 38.
16. Ibid., 39.
17. Ibarra et al., "Women in Leadership," 8.

Acknowledgments

I want to give a special thanks to Jeevan Sivasubramaniam, Managing Director, Editorial, at Berrett-Koehler Publishers. Although Berrett-Koehler did not publish the book, Jeevan believed in the project and introduced me to my literary agent, Rita Rosenkranz. Without his championing this book, it would have been a challenge to find an agent and be published as a first-time author. Thank you, Jeevan!

Many thanks to Rita Rosenkranz for accepting this project and helping me find a publisher almost immediately! Rita, I have great respect for your expertise and knowledge of the industry. I also want to extend a special thanks to my editor, Karen Murphy at Wiley, for believing in the importance of this book and giving me the opportunity to get the message out to professional women who want to move ahead but get lost in the system.

Many thanks, too, to Sophronia Scott for her guidance and support throughout the writing process. Her feedback was invaluable. She helped me find my voice and refine my message. And a special shout out to Laura Baird for her assistance with the graphics and illustrations.

Thank you to the many women who shared their wisdom and graciously gave me their time to be interviewed for this book, including Lois Frankel, Betsy Myers, Marilyn Tam, Timi Hallem, Linda Descano, Carolyn Lawrence, Davia Temin, Chris Reilly, and Linda Tarr-Whelan.

A special thanks to my clients and the many women from my webinars and workshops who responded to my request for interviews and offered their personal stories and lessons learned. Your experiences helped me to create the content of this book.

To my family and friends, thank you so much for cheering me on. Your ongoing support has been wonderful and greatly appreciated. I love you all.

About the Author

Bonnie Marcus, M.Ed. is president of Women's Success Coaching, a company she founded in 2007 to assist professional women in successfully navigating the workplace and advancing their careers. She started her own corporate career at an entry-level position and worked her way up to the top of a national company. With 20-plus years of sales and management experience, Bonnie's extensive business background includes being president/CEO of a ServiceMaster company, and VP of Sales at Medical Staffing Network and at two other national companies in the health care and software industries. She has held executive positions in startup companies and Fortune 500 firms.

As an award-winning entrepreneur, a contributing writer for *Forbes* and *Business Insider*, and a much sought-after professional speaker, Bonnie shares her message globally through keynote speeches, live workshops, blogging, and her popular podcasts. Her passion is to help high-achieving women embrace their ambition and realize their leadership potential.

Forbes.com honored Women's Success Coaching three years in a row as one of the Top 100 Websites for Professional Women, stating, "Women's Success Coaching weighs in on the many building blocks of empowering women in business, from assertive communication to self-promotion to sensitivity training."

Bonnie received a BA in Sociology from Connecticut College and a M.Ed. from New York University. Her website is www.Womens SuccessCoaching.com, and she can be reached by e-mail at Bonnie@ WomensSuccessCoaching.com and on Twitter as @selfpromote. Read her posts on Forbes.com at www.forbes.com/sites/bonniemarcus.

Index